The Mythology of Self Worth

If you want to know how ....

Taming the Black Dog
*How to beat depression – A practical manual for sufferers,
their relatives and colleagues*

Learning to Counsel
Develop the skills you need to counsel others

Never Get Lost Again
*Help is just around the corner for the directionally
challenged*

365 Steps to Self-Confidence
*A programme for personal transformation in just a few
minutes a day*

howtobooks
Send for a free copy of the latest catalogue:
How To Books
3 Newtec Place, Magdalen Road,
Oxford OX4 1RE, United Kingdom
email: info@howtobooks.co.uk
http://www.howtobooks.co.uk

The Mythology of Self Worth

Using reason to dispel the fallacies that trigger
needless anxiety, depression and anger

RICHARD L. FRANKLIN

howtobooks

Published by How To Books Ltd,
3 Newtec Place, Magdalen Road,
Oxford OX4 1RE, United Kingdom
Tel: (01865) 793806 Fax: (01865) 248780
info@howtobooks.co.uk
www.howtobooks.co.uk

First edition 2004

British Library Cataloguing in Publication Data.
A catalogue record for this book is available from
the British Library.

Produced for How To Books by Deer Park Productions, Tavistock
Typeset by Pantek Arts Ltd, Maidstone, Kent
Printed and bound in Great Britain by Bell & Bain Ltd., Glasgow

NOTE: The material contained in this book is set out in good faith for general
guidance and no liability can be accepted for loss or expense incurred as a result of
relying in particular circumstances on statements made in this book. Laws and
regulations are complex and liable to change, and readers should check the current
position with the relevant authorities before making personal arrangements.

Contents

Foreword

Richard L. Franklin has been a pioneering teacher and counsellor of Rational-Emotive Behavior Therapy (REBT) and has naturally gravitated to it through his interest in philosophy and general semantics. This book is the culmination of his work with REBT and is one of the few volumes devoted significantly to self-worth issues. It is a valuable contribution to the self-help field, and those who read it and carefully follow its remarkably clean and well-written presentations will likely considerably help themselves with the many follies related to the common habit of self-rating.

As I was creating and developing the theory and practice of REBT between 1953 and 1955, and as I started to use it from 1955 onward, I was importantly influenced by Paul Tillich, Alfred Korzybski, and Robert Hartman — all of whom realized that rating or measuring one's self or ego leads to emotional disturbance. Following their lead, I looked for destructive self-rating in my early REBT clients and saw that it was rampant among almost all of them. I also realized that it is largely the human condition not to sensibly and sanely evaluate one's performances in order to remain alive and happy, but to irrationally and foolishly give a global rating to one's self, one's essence, and one's being thereby making oneself neurotic.

So as I developed REBT, I showed my clients, my audiences, and the readers of my articles and books, how to unconditionally accept themselves in two main ways. First, they can define themselves as 'good' or 'worthwhile' just because they are human, because they are alive, and because they choose to consider themselves 'worthy' or 'deserving' to remain alive and to enjoy themselves. Second, they can refuse to give their self any global or general rating (which is bound to be inaccurate) and only rate or measure their deeds and acts as 'good' (useful and helpful) or 'bad' (harmful) to their goals and purposes.

Carl Rogers and other existential thinkers often adopt a similar therapeutic approach, but rational-emotive behavior therapy not only shows therapists how to model and use this approach with their clients but also how to actively-directively teach these clients to think about and act on the wisdom of unconditional self-acceptance and to unconditionally accept, and never damn, other human beings.

That is why Richard Franklin's book is so good. He is a remarkably fine teacher of how people think, feel, and behave to either hinder or help themselves and their associates. He zeros in with precision and skill on their crooked thinking and self-defeating feelings and shows them how to use empirical, logical, and metaphorical reasoning to help themselves change.

In addition to their tackling the crucial problem of unconditional self-acceptance, which he returns to several times in this book, he also nicely gets to the common human problems of perfectionism, grandiosity, the dire need for approval, low frustration tolerance, compulsive eating and drinking, purposelessness, and other neurotic conditions. As ever, the solutions he presents are hardheaded, realistic, and devoid of mystical claptrap. This book will hardly solve all your emotional and behavioural problems. But it sure can help!

Albert Ellis, PhD President Albert Ellis Institute,
45 65th Street New York, NY 10021–6593.

Introduction

As I set about preparing this revised and updated version of my original volume, which was entitled *Overcoming the Myth of Self-Worth*, I find there is very little in this section that needs changing; so I'm preserving nearly all of my original words as written over a decade ago on November 17, 1993.

During the 1960s, I found myself at a large Midwestern university teaching an interdisciplinary course in the Humanities Program. At that time, students were demanding that college courses have more relevance to their lives — a demand I had always considered reasonable. Accordingly, I began examining what I was teaching to see how it could be more closely connected to the lives of my students.

My task turned out to be easy. The course I was teaching focused on the contrast between rational belief and belief by faith. I merely had to show how rational thinking could effectively enhance one's life. Needless to say, I found copious examples of how destructive irrational thinking can be and how beneficial rational thinking can be.

I made it a rule to explain logical fallacies using examples from everyday life. I tried to show how fallacy X affected marital communications, how fallacy Y affected one's work, how fallacy Z affected one's sex life, and so forth. Class discussions soon were filled with energy. My classes became so popular, I had to hold them in a small auditorium to accommodate the influx of visitors.

Since my approach was interdisciplinary, I found myself mixing materials from psycholinguistics, analytic philosophy, general semantics, informal logic, and so forth. All the while, I became increasingly aware of how devastating irrational thinking can be in all areas of one's life.

Some years after this experience, a friend asked me to help manage a one-day workshop being put on by an obscure little place called the Rational-Emotive Education Center. The speaker for the workshop was to be Dr Albert Ellis, a psychologist from New York City.

After helping out with registrations, I listened to Dr Ellis's lectures throughout the morning. By noon, my excitement was feverish. For the first time, I was hearing a clear exposition of what I had believed for years: irrational thinking has a profoundly negative effect on one's emotional life.

At lunchtime, I found myself seated across from Dr Ellis. My mind was a whirlpool of thoughts, and I hardly knew where to begin. I bombarded the poor man with endless questions.We chatted about Marcus Aurelius, Bertrand Russell, and Noam Chomsky. We wandered through analytic philosophy, informal logic, and religion. As we concluded, Dr Ellis suggested I spend some time exploring the ways in which Rational-Emotive Behavior Therapy (REBT) overlapped with what I had once taught in my university classes.

Following this pivotal meeting, I joined the staff of the Rational-Emotive Education Center as a trainee and observer. Eventually, I began leading support groups and helping to put on workshops.

The work I had done for several years at the university coalesced beautifully with REBT. I found myself frequently using materials from my former college classes to make points in my REBT support groups. The overlap fascinated me.

This book is the result of that fascination. My intention has been to interweave the materials I used as a humanities teacher with the work of Dr Ellis. The painful question I've been forced to face is whether or not I've added enough to his vast body of distinguished work to justify another REBT self-help book. I'm acutely sensitive to the fact that a plethora of books have been written that seem to be rewritten versions of books already published by Dr Ellis.

After some soul-searching, I concluded that I could offer a somewhat different approach and that I had developed heuristic tools that would be useful to both counsellors and beginners in Rational Self-Counselling. After I finished a rough first draft of my manuscript, I mailed it to Dr Ellis, who responded with an encouraging letter of support. His comments put my doubts to rest, and I went forward with my efforts to publish this modest volume.

I believe this is a good epoch in which to publish this book. For many years, we have been seeing an explosion in self-esteem psychology, a movement that has been metaphysically conceived and ideologically driven. I believe there is much in this misguided movement that is both superstitious and destructive. I hope this book will, in some small measure, help to counteract the mythology being peddled by the self-esteem hucksters.

As you read this book, you may be bemused by and also curious about the many colorful characters with alliterative names populating these pages. They are real people or composites of real people. Most of them are people I've worked with in support groups. I have invented no thoughts or purely fictional beings. These people and their thoughts are real, outlandish though they may seem at times.

A female proofreader protested that 'too many of the characters are women'. This merely reflects the fact that 90% of the members of my support groups were women. I chose each case study only because it clearly illustrated a specific type of fallacious thinking. Gender was irrelevant in nearly all cases.

When all is said and done, this book would never have been possible without the work of Dr Albert Ellis. The foundation stones are pure REBT, and I owe a great intellectual debt to Dr Ellis. I believe we both will be long gone before history finally acknowledges the full impact of his pioneering work, but I honestly believe psychotherapy will one day be seen as B.E. and A.E. — before Ellis and after Ellis.

Richard L. Franklin, Appleton, Wisconsin.

Comments on The Mythology of Self-Worth

By applying the findings of several kinds of psychological research, this splendid book will enable readers to teach themselves how to become more effective in pursuing their own objectives.

Antony Lewis, internationally renowned philosopher, teacher, and author.

In that many problems of everyday living are those of self-proving, this book is especially noteworthy. The author clearly explains the futility and emotional hazards that accompany trying to find something that doesn't exist – human worth and the ego heavens often sought. His instructions for avoiding the self-measurement trap are concisely written, leaving the reader with a more hopeful road map to follow en route to more emotional wellbeing via unconditional self-acceptance. This book is thoughtfully and provocatively written with many practical suggestions for teaching yourself to overreact less and accept yourself more in spite of adversity. The Mythology of Self-Worth is very much 'worth' its reading weight in gold!

Bill Borcherdt, ACSW, BCD, psychotherapist and marital counsellor in Appleton, Wisconsin.

Anyone who has serious self-esteem hangups should, consult Richard L. Franklin's sane little book. Franklin does a superb job of destroying the mythology surrounding the common problems of perfectionism, grandiosity, the dire need for approval, compulsions of all sorts, purposelessness, and neurotic depression. Franklin also reminds us that effective psychotherapy is ultimately a process of self-help. A counsellor can guide the process, but the person seeking change must ultimately use the information he is given to revamp his dysfunctional thinking.

Robert Baker, Professor Emeritus of Psychology, University of Kentucky, noted author of several books, and Fellow of CSICOP who has often appeared on national TV as a sceptic regarding claims of the paranormal.

1

You and Your Emotion-Brain

6 Chastise thy passions that they not avenge themselves upon thee. 9

Epictetus

Three hundred and sixty-five million years ago a strange creature called a crossopterygian first left its watery home. Propelled by bony fins, it flopped pathetically onto land. As it made this slithering emergence from the primeval sea, it did so under the direction of a tiny brain stem — a laughably small organ that, nonetheless, did its job. It unthinkingly controlled breathing, digestion, and excretion. This ancient reptilian brain is found today in all vertebrates, and it still does essentially the same job.

Millions of years passed. Then, in the age of the giant reptiles, warm-blooded mammals appeared. By about 25 million BC, monkeys were swinging through the trees. In these early primates, we see a new brain at work — the paleomammalian — a brain that remains much the same in all mammals to this day. Burgeoning upward and around the brain stem, it would become a cauldron for rage and grief, for lust and terror. In man we sometimes call it the old brain or the emotion-brain.

On the foundation of the emotion-brain, and just beneath the bony carapace of the skull, the final evolution of man's triune

1

brain took place. A convoluted grey tissue enveloped the old brain like a swelling cupola. A deep fissure cleaved this jellylike tissue, thereby creating hemispheres and truly giving man two minds.

To the left side was given the task of language, of analysis, of taking apart and figuring out. To the right side was given our sense of space and pattern, of proportions and wholes. It is with the left side that we examine the pieces of a jigsaw puzzle. It is with the right side that we envision the whole picture. While the left side spells out the words of poetry, the right side hears their music. These two halves form what we call man's new brain — his thinking brain.

This book is concerned with the mysterious communication between your thinking brain and your emotion-brain, about a conversation that profoundly affects how you feel and act. In short, it's about the art of self-talk. You will learn that what you

say to your emotion-brain spawns the vital difference between rage and disappointment, between anxiety and concern, between sadness and depression. Your self-talk will determine whether you will enjoy the game of life or be tormented by

> This book is concerned with the mysterious communication between your thinking brain and your emotion-brain.

every setback, whether you will have a happy love life or be forever looking.

This language skill will not come easily. You will need patience and discipline. And hard work. You will need to master dozens of subtleties in language and thought to communicate efficiently with your hard-to-reach emotion-brain. Sometimes I call our old brain Dummibrain, not because it is stupid, but because *it is linguistically naïve.* You see, Dummibrain was given neither the gift of language nor the capacity to recognize delicate nuances. It is this naïvete that makes our self-talk perilous and threatens to throw us into darkest gloom or sabotage cherished goals.

Your old brain is better at preparing you for fight or flight. It easily gets lost in the tangled labyrinth of words and syntax. It is often pathetic at translating metaphors or tempering simple exaggerations. Dummibrain does best with messages such as, *This is bad for me. This is good for me. This is dangerous. This person is my enemy.* When, however, we go beyond this simplicity and take flight on wings of poetry, we may easily mystify Dummibrain. He is stubbornly literal about words.

A simple phrase such as *I can't stand it!* can be an alarm bell galvanizing Dummibrain into pushing your panic button. To Dummibrain, these words may mean your survival is at stake, while to your thinking brain they are only a figure of speech. When you say, 'I can't live without him' you may confuse your emotion-brain. If you tell yourself you *can't stand* rejection, the thought may act as a signal you're facing imminent danger.

Once Dummibrain pushes your fear button, your body will be triggered into making dramatic preparations. Your eyes will dilate. Your blood will flow from your stomach to major muscles. Your heart will beat rapidly, contract strongly. Your bronchial tubes will open. Blood pressure will rise. Muscles will tense. All of this is to prepare you for the 'danger' of rejection when you ask somebody for a date or try to strike up a conversation with a stranger.

At this point, Dummibrain is in the saddle, controlling your bodily reactions and overriding your thinking brain in your choice of action. You avoid asking that attractive redhead for a date — her rejection would be too 'dangerous'. You drop out of a course — the final exam is too 'dangerous'. This ignoble flight can devastate your personal growth.

There is no doubt about it — Dummibrain can be your enemy. And he is a formidable foe. Once he leaps into action, he can be overpowering. He can drag you into despair or terrorize you over life's everyday frustrations.

Dummibrain is better at preparing you for fight or flight. He can be easily misled by words or thoughts. Words such as 'My boss is killing me' can lead to primitive and wholly inappropriate anger.

But take heart, these painful experiences are not inevitable. This book
will equip you with self-talk you can
use to tame your emotion-brain, a
specialized problem-solving language

> There is no doubt about it — Dummibrain can be your enemy.

that disentangles the snares of words and thinking that trigger
inappropriate emotions.

This is not a language you will always want to use. It is life-
less and dull and is meant to be activated only when you face
problems in your life. Some will need it only for major crises,
others will need it for everyday frustrations. How much you will
have need of this finely chiselled self-talk will depend on how
word-reactive your emotion-brain is, on how much nutty thinking you learned as a child, and how fast you unlearn old habits.

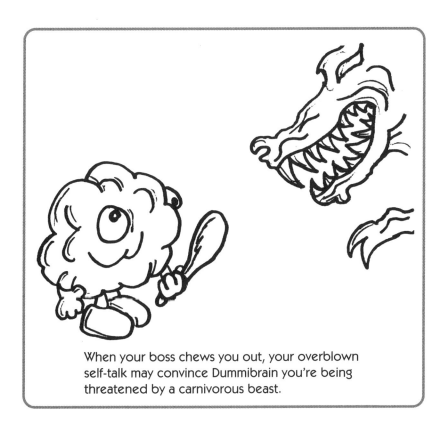

When your boss chews you out, your overblown
self-talk may convince Dummibrain you're being
threatened by a carnivorous beast.

Your new talk will be a powerful tool. It will not, however, make you feel happy when you suffer a loss in your life. It will not weave positive

Your new talk will be a powerful tool.

feelings on a loom of negative events. Your new self-talk will simply teach you how to be less upset. You will learn how to keep your emotion-brain from freezing you with anxiety or numbing you with depression. Through carefully crafted self-talk, you will learn to contain your emotional storms.

This control over your emotion-brain can yield a cornucopia of benefits. It can help you cut down on nicotine, sugar, alcohol, and caffeine — mood elevators you use to manage your emotions. Rather than light up when you're nervous, you can switch to self-talk that calms you. Rather than pour a shot when you're angry, you can use language designed to mollify your overly excited emotion-brain. Rather than eat chocolate when you feel blue, you can coax Dummibrain into giving you more get-up-and-go.

Sometimes we narcotize ourselves with television, trashy novels, sleeping, or endless hours on the phone. These all have one thing in common: they are distractive. They switch off the self-talk that is stirring up the emotion-brain. These methods often seem to work well, but only as stopgap remedies. You may temporarily *feel* better, but you will fail to *get* better.

Short-term distractions fail in the long run because they ignore the core problem: how to attack and replace your hurtful self-talk scripts. These are scripts you've practised for many years, possibly dating back to the age of seven or eight. With no alternative self-talk, you will compulsively use these old, defective scripts to take measure of the negative events in your life.

As human beings, we are strongly evaluative creatures. When facing an event, we measure it, form some idea of whether it's bad or good for us, and then act accordingly. This habit is part of our survival kit. Without vigilance and a constant measuring of the dangers in our environment, our species would never have survived.

Unfortunately, our skills at accurately measuring the actual threats in our modern world have not evolved along with the rise of civilization. Our emotion-brain did this job fairly well many thousands of years ago, but it simply is not equipped to make sound judgments regarding many of the problems of life in the modern world. Alas, we humans often tend to stir up wildly inappropriate emotions as we seek to deal with the ubiquitous frustrations of our everyday lives.

So what's the answer? The solution to this senseless emotional turmoil is not to narcotize ourselves with the multiple distractions offered by modern society; the answer lies in replacing ineffective self-talk that can rein in our emotion-brain when it runs amok. What we need is a new discourse — a self-talk that uses facts, not supposition; logic not contradiction; probability, not possibility.

So what's the answer?

If your left brain fails to speak with a clear voice, your primitive brain may misunderstand and trigger an emotional storm. This may have been useful when our ancient ancestors faced saber-toothed tigers, but it's almost always out of place in modern society. When your boss chews you out, you're not facing a saber-toothed tiger. The result of misplaced self-talk may be behaviour that is all out of proportion. Unfortunately, while you're cowering before imaginary tigers or hiding from them, your real problem lies unattended.

Your left brain often fails to speak clearly because of simple clumsiness, bald-faced contradiction, or gross exaggeration. Another part of the communication gap results from the way we store our ideas and memories. The human brain seems to have two memory boxes: one for long-term memory and one for short-term memory. The beliefs we store in our long-term memory box may start out as verbatim sentences, but they eventually become highly condensed. These compressed thoughts can be encoded in brief signals transmitted in microseconds.

These flashed signals tend to lurk on the periphery of our thinking, and we seldom notice them; nonetheless, they are being sent, and Dummibrain hears them. How is it we can hear, but not hear? Or see, but not see? I'm not sure, but it does happen. Have you ever had the odd experience of running across an old friend, staring directly at him, and still not seeing him?

You were seeing him, but not seeing him. His image was some-how present in your brain, but you weren't paying any attention to what your optic nerve was registering.

Thoughts can be like that. We can think thoughts that dance on the edge of consciousness where we fail to notice them; how-ever, we can also learn to detect these flashed signals. And once we tune in on them, we can decipher them. We can even commit the decoded words and sentences to paper. As you gain in this skill, you will find that what passes for knee-jerk emotional reac-tions are actually reactions to compressed inner talk — a one-way conversation you long ago stopped paying any attention to.

You will be acting as a kind of detective as you sharpen your tracking skills. You'll learn to look at the evidence of your own behaviour and feelings and then trace them back to the con-densed messages you habitually send to Dummibrain. As you unmask this 'hidden' part of your self talk, you will put yourself in a position to articulate it, attack it, and replace it.

This task can seem daunting. You will have to work hard to overcome your inner-talk habits. You've practised these habits for years, and they will not be easily con-quered. You'll find that the new self-talk I recommend to you will feel unnatural. At times it will seem as unnatural as writing with your left hand if you're right-handed.

> **This task can seem daunting.**

Don't let that worry you. *Natural* merely refers to a feeling you get after you've practised something for a long time. After you've used your new self-talk for several months, it will slowly begin to feel comfortable. In fact, it will ultimately seem more natural than your old talk because it will make more sense.

Abnormal, like *unnatural*, is another word that gets kicked around. It's probably quite normal to feel scared about speaking before a group. But would you choose insomnia, a tension headache, or a churning stomach just because it's normal to feel that way? *Normal* merely refers to what most of the people do most of the time. Most of the people in our society put them-selves through a lot of unnecessary anger, anxiety, and depression. If this is normal, who wants to be normal? This book is a manual on how to be abnormal!

Along with all the humbug we hear about what's *natural* and what's *normal*, we often hear the platitude, *Trust your feelings*. In other words, let your gut reaction tell you what to do. Nonsense. That is some of the worst bilge ever concocted by New Age irrationality.

Let me give you a convincing example borrowed from Dr Maxie Maultsby. Suppose you are an American going to England for a vacation. As you fly across the Atlantic, you worry about having to drive on the left side of the road. To get

> Let me give you a convincing example borrowed from Dr Maxie Maultsby.

yourself in the right mind-set, you keep telling yourself, 'Once I'm in an English car, I've got to focus on staying on the left side of the road. If I don't, I may get myself hurt or killed.' These are eminently rational, sensible thoughts. Not feelings, mind you, but *thoughts*.

Yet after all this mental preparation, once you get in your British car and start driving down the left lane, it will *feel* absolutely wrong to you. Your bodily feedback will keep urging you to move over into the right lane. The lesson is clear. Your feelings may point you toward death or destruction if you follow their urgings. Trust your feelings? Humbug.

If you are going to ignore such promptings and think more rationally, you will need to learn some elementary logic. Not the fancy, complicated stuff they call symbolic logic, but something called informal logic. This is a powerful tool. It enables you to see if a belief is daffy simply by examining your self-talk. In other words, you won't have to examine the world outside your head to see if a thought is daffy.

The second tool you will need is the empirical method. This is the method scientists use. First you uncover a common belief showing up in your self-talk. Then you look at all the evidence

> The second tool you will need is the empirical method.

counting for the belief and all the evidence counting against the belief. If considerable evidence counts against your belief, and very little counts for it, you know it needs re-examination.

It will be crucial for you to use the empirical method in building your self-talk. All too often, we tell ourselves things that have no factual support — superstitious thoughts that set off many of our emotional tempests.

Does it seem overstated when I say *superstitious thoughts*? After all, you're a civilized person living in the twenty-first century. You know darn well you're not superstitious. Nonetheless, let's put you to the test. I'll ask you a few questions, and you try to come up with honest answers.

Would you ever feel anxious about asking an attractive stranger for a dance? About speaking before a large group? About taking a final exam? Would you ever get angry if somebody called you a nasty name? If your new car broke down on a vacation trip? If you were stuck for an hour in a traffic jam? Would you ever get depressed if you were turned down for a date? If you failed a final exam? If you lost out on a promotion? If you answered yes to any of these, you are almost certainly using some superstitious self-talk.

Don't get me wrong. You would be wise to be concerned about an important final exam. And it's certainly not nutty to get annoyed when your new car breaks down. Nor would it be overreacting to feel disappointed when you lose out on a promotion. But these milder emotions — concern, annoyance, and disappointment — seldom last long. More importantly, they won't block you from getting what you want out of life. Sadness or disappointment won't sap your vitality or rob you of sleep — depression will. Annoyance won't make you take it out on your kids or employees — anger will. Concern won't block you from experimenting with new things or meeting new people — anxiety will.

I hope you can see I'm not talking about positive thinking. I won't try to bamboozle you into thinking positively about negative events in your life. That kind of thinking rarely works for the

> I hope you can see I'm not talking about positive thinking.

simple reason it asks us to believe what is not believable. Trying to indoctrinate yourself with baseless beliefs is a Pollyanna approach that collapses with time.

What I'm talking about is a form of self-talk that gets its power from logic and evidence — the twin pillars of truth and believability. By using this solid underpinning, you will happily find that your new self-talk is far more believable than some of the rubbish you are probably telling yourself. I can promise you that you'll find this approach more reliable than positive thinking.

By learning some simple, practical uses of logic and evidence, you will become a scientist busily cleaning out the clutter of superstition in your mental laboratory. You will undertake a journey that will be both exciting and heretical. I will invite you to challenge time-encrusted ideas that have haunted and disturbed human beings for thousands of years. Stay with me, and together we will jettison much of the prevailing mythology of modern psychotherapy and self-help literature.

You will be coming face-to-face with radical ideas on self-worth, love and hate, cause and effect, good and evil, and basic human needs. I hope some of the heresies I pose for you will entertain you. Some may astonish you. Others may trigger your anger. But if you stay with me, I doubt that you will be bored, and I believe you will learn a powerful system for taking control of your life.

Now let's tackle what is arguably the most powerful, ubiquitous, and destructive myth of all.

2

The Myth of Self-Worth

6 Let the ghosts go. We will worship them no more. Let
them cover their eyeless sockets with their fleshless
hands and fade forever from the imaginations of
men. 9

Robert G. Ingersoll

Honour, decency, worthiness. Behind such lofty words lies a grim history of carnage and suffering — a history of the struggle between honour and dishonour, between good and evil, between the worthy and the unworthy. Man has desperately fought and struggled to be worthy of his race, tribe, or religion. He has willingly sacrificed his life rather than surrender his self-worth. And he has mindlessly extinguished the lives of those he has deemed worthless. Vast numbers of Jews, gays, gypsies, Armenians, and alleged witches have been slaughtered because they have been seen as lacking human worth.

For these reasons, I think we should concern ourselves about what we mean by human worth. After all, there is almost a universal belief in the existence of this quality — a belief that self-worth is both real and essential for every human being. You may have your own word for this arcane quality, this mysterious entity that seems to be more precious than life itself. I choose to call it self-worth.

I will be focusing on the concept of self-worth as it relates to personal growth and happiness. At this level, the belief in self-worth has caused more emotional suffering and more self-destructive acts than any other belief fashioned by the human mind. Its ghostly presence haunts almost all our most pernicious self-talk. It is a ubiquitous and pervasive malignancy, and I want to excise it at once.

Allow me to begin with the most obvious question: What is the meaning of the term **self-worth**? How do we define it? Somehow we have to reach an agreement as to what we're talking about when we use this term. As you will see, this is no easy task. I'm reminded of the time I was leading a support group, and a woman furiously insisted she had self-worth — albeit she didn't know what it was. Unwilling to even discuss the issue, she caustically suggested I look up self-worth in the dictionary if I didn't know what it was. I guess I got told.

> Allow me to begin with the most obvious question.

I'm sorry to say this is a common piece of nonsense believed by most people: if you want to know what something is, look it up in the dictionary. But dictionaries, alas, will not tell us what a thing *is* — they merely give us equivalent words. If you look up *June bug*, the dictionary will tell you it is a large leaf-eating Melolonthidae. So what have you learned? You have learned that the word beetle refers to the same object as June bug, and you also know the Latin word used by scientists. You still, however, do not know what a June bug *is*.

To help remedy this, many dictionaries include photographs or drawings to show you what a word refers to. Admittedly, this works well for concrete objects. But what about abstract words? How about justice? Or democracy? Or bigotry? You can't exactly draw a picture of these or even point to them. True, you can point to a jury at work, a ballot box, or a lynching. These are things that accompany *justice, democracy* and *bigotry*. This gives us some help by at least loosely connecting words to something objective.

But some words defy even this treatment. How about the word *hooray*? We can't point to it anywhere in the world. There is no *thing* it refers to. We can only describe the way the word is used. What we usually do is make up rules for using such words.

As you can see, a dictionary isn't the answer to our problem. Having said that, let's energetically tackle the term self-worth. Let's see if we can ultimately craft a serviceable definition. To do so, let's begin our investigation by considering what self-worth refers to. In other words, we can start with an inventory of the furniture of the world so as to see which objects (if any) self-worth points to. Alas, when we try this, we find that it does not seem to refer to any *thing* whatsoever. In fact, we could traipse all over the globe and never find a specimen of self-worth that we might describe, collect, measure, weigh, photograph, or whatever.

Having failed with that approach, let's try a second method. If there are no *things* in the world that self-worth refers to, can we find some concrete objects that go with self-worth in the way a ballot box goes with democracy? At first glance, this approach seems promising, but we are quickly disabused of our hopes when we start looking. We find ourselves bogged down in a quicksand of conflicting opinions. Most of us can agree that a ballot box is a concrete sign of democracy. But signs of self-worth? We find ourselves in a jungle without a map.

If we watch people scrambling for self-worth, we see them pursuing an incredible diversity of things: a mink coat, a new Rolls Royce, a gorgeous lover, a diploma, a nice physique, even a posthumous medal. The more we look, the more we come to see that people value thousands of things as outward signs of self-worth. Clearly, this method will get us nowhere. We are still left wondering what self-worth *is*.

Not to worry. There is an excellent third method for determining the meanings of words. We can closely observe how speakers of Standard English use the locution self-worth. Such observations enable us to make a list of rules on how to use the term. In other words, we can build what is often referred to as a descriptive definition because it is based on how and when people actually use this slippery word.

Not to worry.

Aha! We soon discover a mountain of evidence showing us how people actually use the term self-worth. If we take a poll among psychologists, counsellors, sociologists, and so forth, we learn that two signs supposedly indicate the presence of self-worth. You have self-worth when (1) you have love or approval, or (2) you perform well. It is only then that we tell ourselves we are worthy human beings.

Despite vast clinical evidence that this is what self-worth means in actual usage, most people still stubbornly insist there is some mystical entity above and beyond winning approval or performing well. They claim it is this spectre that is referred to when we talk about self-worth.

Don't swallow this. This belief is pure superstition — a piece of mumbo-jumbo that can devastate your growth if you don't

Don't swallow this.

uproot it from your world view. *There is no such thing as self-worth*. You may longingly tell yourself you possess this ghostly chimera, but your protests will not conjure it into existence.

Take my word for it — there are no workable ways to rate the worth of a human being. Philosophers have sought the answer to this conundrum for 2,000 years with pitiful results. You can rate your behaviour because we have yardsticks for measuring performance. But rate your personhood? Don't waste your time. It's a fool's quest, a quixotic journey to nowhere.

It seems that nowadays gaining a sense of self-worth is the Holy Grail of the self-esteem movement. What a foolish search. Worth versus non-worth, self-esteem versus lack of self-esteem — these and other revered notions of psychobabble are far too mercurial to define a human being. It's a slippery path that leads us nowhere.

Bertrand Russell, the great English philosopher, was the first to give us clues on how this dead-end street leads us to nonsense. He called it a *category mistake*. He pointed out that words belong to distinct families, and you can end up talking gibberish if you mix separate groups.

For example, the words *triangle* and *platypus* belong to different categories. If I say something like, 'Triangles copulate with platypuses', I'm saying something senseless. After much reflection, I long ago decided that *worth* and *self* are as far apart as platypuses and triangles. They clearly belong in discrete categories. I'm convinced the sentence, 'I'm a worthless person', is, at bottom, a blatant category mistake.

This muddleheaded linking of self and worth might be fairly harmless if it didn't hook up with another batty idea, namely: I must have self-worth. Without self-worth, I'll be worthless, a loser, a zero. Just imagine how this self-talk sounds to your emotion-brain.

Remember that Dummibrain is dreadfully naïve about words. He'll take this bunkum literally. He is mainly concerned with your survival and has little appreciation for the subtleties of language. If he thinks you might be reduced to a zero, for example, he'll hit the panic button. Consider what Dummibrain is hearing. Becoming a nothing sounds as though you're facing death or extinction. Your emotion-brain sees this as a dangerous situation with survival at stake.

Does this sound farfetched to you? If you doubt me, consider the panic people feel when facing possible rejection. Dr Paul Hauck loves to quote the story of **Does this sound farfetched to you?** John Alden and Miles Standish. Standish was a courageous military man who had no qualms about risking his life to fight hostile Indians. Nonetheless, he was terrified at the thought Priscilla Mullens might reject him. For Standish, her words of rejection could be more dangerous than a host of arrows from Indian warriors.

Look around you. This kind of fear is rampant in our society. Many would opt for whitewater canoeing, hang gliding, sky **Look around you.** diving, or going over Niagara Falls in a barrel rather than speak before a group. I've known men who would rather fight Muhammad Ali in his prime than introduce themselves to a woman at a dance. These quavering men seem to think they face a slippery slope that goes like this:

rejection = being diminished = becoming nothing = non-survival.

To uproot this superstitious and muddled attitude once and for all, you must eventually uncover and excise your underlying belief in self-worth. This, in turn, means giving up the fruitless search for self-esteem.

Have you ever thought about what *self-esteem* means? It literally means to esteem or judge the self — a truly foolhardy enterprise. Nowadays we are deluged with exhortations from the so-called self-esteem movement. From pulpit, press, and podium, we are urged to build our self-esteem and to teach our children to do the same.

Unfortunately, no effective tools are ever provided for doing so. The result is predictable — people fall back on trying to build their self-esteem through outstanding performance or winning lavish approval. Self-esteem becomes a *de facto* slavish courting of the esteem of others and self-defeating perfectionism at work and play.

Trying to build self-esteem is like wandering lost in the Gobi Desert without a map or compass. There are no valid guidelines for judging the value of a human being. The pursuit of self-esteem will only lead to a dead end. One ends up focusing obsessively on one's **self**. Paradoxically, people who focus on the self don't get very far — they only become self-centred.

Have you ever thought about the term *self-centred*? It means placing the self at the centre of your focus. If you worry constantly about building self-esteem or whether you have self-worth, you soon become a self-centred bore.

> **Have you ever thought about the term self-centred?**

Self-centred people are running scared. They're afraid of being rejected, afraid of making mistakes, afraid of being diminished. Happy people are **problem**-centred, not **self**-centred. They're not worried about building self-confidence. Think about it. How the devil can you have confidence in a *self*?

To understand this, list ten things you have confidence in. For example: 'I have confidence I can do a vertical jump of 20 inches'. And so forth. At the end of the list add, 'I have confidence in my self'. Study your list. You see what I mean? You've written nine things that make sense and one item that is basically senseless.

What is truly useful is to face your problems. This is what gives you control over your life. For this kind of orientation, you don't need a mystical, unobtainable self-confidence. You will, however, want to build other kinds of confidence. Two types are crucial — rejection-coping confidence and failure-coping confidence. You will need these skills to convince yourself you can make mistakes or face disapproval without falling apart. In the coming pages, I will show you how to fashion these tools and make them a part of your self-talk toolbox.

Once you've learned to focus on your problems rather than your self, your emotional life will become much smoother. Self-worth seekers are not only running scared; they're usually riding an emotional roller coaster. When Betty's lover is giving her strokes, Betty is riding high. When he ignores her or seems distracted, she's moody and irritable. She's on a downswing.

Or take the case of Mike. When Mike plays tennis and wins, he's elated. He feels like he's king of the mountain. But look out when he loses. He sinks into an ugly black mood that makes his kids clear out of the house and his dog hide under the bed.

Emotionally speaking, Betty and Mike are yo-yos. They go up and down according to how well they do at work or play. When Mike plays tennis he focuses on **how well** he is doing — not on **what** he is doing. He is violating a vital dictum for the good life; for if you want to be fulfilled and happy, you must focus on what you are doing, not on how well you are doing. I suggest you memorize these words: *I will strive to focus on* **what** *I am doing, not on* **how well** *I am doing.* Write this motto on a sheet of paper, then frame it and hang it where you see it every day of your life.

Obsession with how well you are doing can eat away at life's every pleasure. It's a cancer that disfigures even the simplest beauties of life. A woman in one of my

> Obsession with how well you are doing can eat away at life's every pleasure.

support groups whined to the group that she had been unable to enjoy a spectacular Pacific sunset. Why? Because she had nobody to share it with. The pathos of her self-talk is found in a submerged rhetorical question, 'What good is beauty if you can't share it with a special someone?'

Sam offers us another example of these lost souls. Whenever he makes love to Mabel, his self-talk sounds like this: 'I wonder if I'm really turning her on. Did I spend enough time on foreplay? I wonder if she'll have a climax. What if she doesn't? Will she think I'm a lousy lover? Suppose she decides to look for a new boyfriend. I hope I can stay hard. She'll really think I'm a wimp if I lose my erection. Damn! I think I climaxed too soon.'

Guess what. One day Sam finds he can't get an erection. Is it any wonder? He's so worried about how well he's doing; he does not even notice how good sex feels. He's blocking himself from delicious sensations, and the joy of sex is withering along with his erection.

What Sam lacks is not virility, but rational self-talk. He needs a new script based on reality. With a sane script, he would be telling himself it's no big deal if he doesn't perform like Super Stud, that he can handle it when he doesn't do well, that he's a fallible human being who will never function perfectly. That's the kind of self-talk that will build his failure-coping confidence and reinvigorate his enjoyment of sex.

Sam may need an X-rated script to recharge his sex life. Sexy feelings come from sexy thoughts. If Sam talks to himself about what he's feeling instead of how well he's performing, he'll get back in touch with his sexual self. Instead of practising a killjoy script, Sam needs to develop a joy-of-sex script.

Mike uses killjoy self-talk when he plays tennis. On a beautiful spring day, with the birds singing, with the fragrance of lilacs drenching the air, with a warm breeze caressing his skin, with fresh air filling his lungs, with his muscles revelling in movement, Mike is tense and dispirited. He's losing his tennis match. All of the luscious feelings he could be immersing himself in are being obliterated by the agony of defeat.

Mike has become neurotically competitive because he lays his entire value as a human being on the line every time he plays tennis. That's a peculiar trait of self-worth devotees — they surrender their entire self-worth every time they run up against somebody with more skill or knowledge. A risky business, this pursuit of self-worth.

One day, as he plays an older tennis player, Mike starts telling himself something like, *It would be terrible to lose to this guy. Heck, he must be 50 years old. I couldn't stand it if I lost to such an old man. Everybody will think I'm a real zero if I lose this set. I should never lose to a guy twice my age. I simply must beat this guy.* You can see why Mike is feeling tense and anxious.

If Mike ever learned to tune in on his self-talk, he could logically rip his screwy script apart. In quick succession, he could easily knock down each nutty thought. Taking on each sentence one by one, Mike might carry on an internal argument something like the following:

1. Would it be terrible if I lost? What nonsense. It would hardly be terrible. Winning is more fun than losing, but even if I lose, I still can enjoy playing tennis on such a gorgeous day.

2. Would I really be unable to stand it if I lost? What horse manure. Of course I can stand it if I lose. I've lost before, and it didn't kill me, so I must have stood it. True, I may not have stood it very well, but I did stand it. I merely need to work at standing it better when I lose.

3. Would I somehow become a zero if I lost? Good Lord, what an idiotic thought. How could I become a zero? I'm a person, not a cypher.

4. Is it true I should and must beat this guy? That's crazy. After all, if he plays better than I do, he should win — not me. Why should I win if I play poorly and he plays well? If I'm having a bad day, that's tough. I'm a fallible human being, so I have bad days and good days. It's daffy to think life should be any different.

Since there is no viable way for Mike to rate his personhood, he has fallen into a habit common to self-worth worshippers. First he rates his performance. Then he equates himself with his performance. 'Mike is a tennis player' becomes 'Mike = tennis player'. Tennis is not simply something Mikes *does*; Mike literally *is* his tennis playing. The next stage easily follows. Good tennis playing = good Mike; bad tennis playing = bad Mike.

Even our language contributes to this. The 'is' in *Mike is a tennis player*, is sometimes called the 'is' of identity. This includes any form of the verb 'to be'. It makes the two parts of a sentence equal or identical. According to experts in general semantics, if I say *Bob is a plumber*, I actually suggest more than the idea Bob does plumbing, I imply the equation Bob = plumber. Likewise, when Jill says, *I'm a mother*, she implies she does nothing but parenting. General semanticists, psycholinguists, and others have become aware of the subtle ways the *is* of identity affects our emotions. Using the framework of this book, we can say Jill's thinking brain knows perfectly well she does many things other than parenting. Dummibrain, on the other hand, reacts naïvely to the *is* (*am, are, was, were,* and so forth) of identity. He tends to equate *I am a bad mother* with I am a bad person rather than interpreting it as a comment about parenting skills. If you think this theory is off base, just try telling any woman she's a bad mother. You risk provoking a defensive fury that will send you scuttling for cover.

I'm suggesting Mike would be wise to stop using the *is* of identity in his self-talk. He would do well to frequently remind himself tennis is only something he does. This is a wise preparation for when he plays tennis badly. When he has a bad day on the courts, the only thing he'll view as being bad is his tennis playing. Similarly, Jill would be wise to think of parenting as a single skill, only one thing among the many thousands she does. That way, when she does some lousy parenting (something all parents do from time to time), she won't see herself as a louse.

Mike's wife keeps telling him tennis is only a game. We often hear this being said when people take games too seriously. It reflects a common intuition that people sometimes equate their total self with the game they're playing. Some game players seem to be unaware they're much, much more than players of tennis or chess. Oddly enough, a person like Mike might admit to having done a dumb thing at one time or another; yet, he wouldn't use that admission to conclude he was a dumb *person*. Have you ever done a dumb thing? Do you believe that makes you a dumb *person*?

> Have you ever done a dumb thing? Do you believe that makes you a dumb person?

If you get a handle on this distinction, you'll take a big step toward understanding the way you make yourself feel guilty. The basis of all guilt is the failure to separate one's personhood from one's actions. Take a careful look at the kind of self-talk that generates feelings of guilt. You'll find two key sentences: (1) *I did a bad thing, and* (2) *therefore, I am a bad person.*

The first sentence is healthy and useful. If you have done something bad or foolish, it doesn't pay to waste time and effort trying to squirm your way out of your mistake. Admit it. After all, you did it. This will help you to accept your fallibility and to learn from your mistakes.

The second sentence in this tandem is another matter. This is the loony part. Attack this notion by reminding yourself there is no valid way to rate the self. Rationally speaking, we can only rate a given behaviour. Keep telling yourself you're much more than a single behaviour. You do many, many things — some good, some bad, and most of them neutral. If I keep my word to my kid, I normally can rate that as good parenting. If I lie to my spouse, I can usually rate that as bad for our marriage. If I eat toast at breakfast, I can rate that as neither good nor bad.

In short, when you have feelings of guilt, you are going beyond telling yourself you did something bad. You are irrationally adding the notion you're a bad person. Eliminate this added self-blame, and you eliminate your ersatz sense of guilt. It is this gratuitous *non sequitur* that triggers your guilt feelings. You see, Dummibrain is reacting to your senseless equation of badness and self and is stirring up depression or anxiety.

You can immediately sense it when Dummibrain is pushing your buttons because you're flooded with strong physical feelings. As a matter of fact, many people believe these physical feedbacks *are* their emotions. This is a mistaken notion. These are simply physical reactions that typically occur along with certain self-talk scripts. They are secondary spinoffs of your irrational self-talk.

A script with scary thoughts, for example, may make you feel hyper, while another script may make you feel drained of energy. Since the physical feelings always follow the self-talk, you'll find it more efficient to label specific scripts as your actual anger, anxiety, or depression. You'll see how sensible this is when you learn to purge some of your nuttier scripts. As you do, you'll find the resulting physical feelings also disappear. A guilt script, for example, might make you feel dragged out. Replace this inane script with rational thoughts and your energy bounces back.

Mind you, this is not the only benefit you'll gain from overcoming your guilt complex. You'll also be on your way to conquering the 'excuse habit'. Human beings spend astonishing amounts of time and energy trying to worm out of responsibility for their mistakes. Learn to monitor your excuse making. Listen carefully to your self-talk. Do you instantly grope for any excuse you can devise when you goof? Or do you say something like, *Wow! I really blew that one*? If you find you're trying to rig explanations for every mistake you make, or if you're using an excessive amount of energy explaining why it's not your fault when you mess up, you're probably worrying about your precious self-worth.

Excuse making is an ingrained habit that takes hard work to overcome. Don't let mental excuses slip by. Challenge them. Tell yourself, *I did it. I botched the job. Oh well, I guess that proves I'm not perfect. Now let me see, where did I go wrong?*

Suppose you try to fix the leaky drainpipe on your kitchen sink. Further suppose you wreck the pipe and make the leak twice as bad. Don't compose a litany of dumb excuses such as, *I didn't have the right tools. The damned pipe wasn't fixable anyway. It must have been a lousy imported pipe.*

These excuses won't do a thing to make you feel better about your plumbing skills. I know it sounds paradoxical, but if you want to feel better, forcefully announce that you blew it. Use a self-talk script that sounds like this: *Holy Zeus. I really finished off that pipe. I'll never win any awards as a plumber. I should take a picture of this mangled mess and show it to my Uncle Joe, who's a plumber. He'd have a good laugh.* As you practise this kind of self-talk, you'll find it gets infinitely easier to face your mistakes. Eventually, you'll find you can bungle things without getting the least bit angry. Annoyed, yes — angry, no. In fact, you may even learn to laugh at some of your more spectacular goofs.

Often our fear of admitting mistakes is a fear of disapproval. We're afraid to let others see our fallibility. We crazily believe such exposure is a surefire way to lose our self-worth. Be relentless in attacking this nonsense. Keep telling yourself you won't shrink if somebody is critical or laughs at your latest blunder. Act on your new self-talk by telling your friends about your mistakes and gross blunders. Describe your latest goofs with a dose of wry humour. If you learn to laugh a little at your screw-ups, the world will laugh with you — not at you.

> **Often our fear of admitting mistakes is a fear of disapproval.**

Take the example of my friend Bob. This man has a PhD in theoretical physics. He is one of the smartest people I know. He also is one of the most accomplished handypersons I've ever known. Yet, when I visit him, he can't wait to tell me about his latest botches, blunders and bungles. I've heard about his quavering fear of spiders, his knee-knocking fear of heights, his inability to add and subtract, and his ineptness with the English language. And guess what? I always go away with a renewed respect for this man's sanity and strength. We would all do well to emulate his attitude.

Bob doesn't obsessively worry about winning the approval or praise of others. Fear of disapproval can be a heavy albatross. It can shackle you in countless ways. You may develop a fear of trying anything new. You may lose your capacity to sample and enjoy new experiences. You may easily become morbidly haunted by fears of looking foolish. Friends invite you to go roller-skating, but you instinctively say no. You're afraid you'll take a pratfall and look silly. You tell yourself you'll look like a loser, a zero.

It's hardly a surprise these thoughts spook Dummibrain. Hearing these alarming messages, he pulls your anxiety switch. You're flooded with physical feelings of nervousness — feelings that tend to reinforce your fears. *You tell yourself, This doesn't feel right. I feel uncomfortable with the whole idea.* The result is predictable. You hide fearfully at home while your friends are having a good time at the skating rink.

Which is more painful: doing what you fear, or ducking what you fear? Is it really easier to run and hide? Remember: every time you practise avoidance, this process becomes easier. Every time you use an avoidance script, it becomes more ingrained. Soon you become a knee-jerk coward.

Which is more painful: doing what you fear, or ducking what you fear?

If you're a cowardly lion, there's no yellow brick road for you to follow, nor will you find a wizard to help you. The solution lies in ridding yourself of harmful self-talk and creating rational scripts. If you stick to your old fear-provoking self-talk, you may stay for years in a job you detest, frantically hang on to a bad relationship, live your whole life in a city you hate, or forever have a dull sex life. In your anxious pursuit of a ghostly self-worth, you may marry the wrong person, teach school when you'd prefer to be a carpenter, drive a Cadillac when you'd prefer a Mini Cooper, or torment yourself with impractical, uncomfortable clothes.

Mind you, trashing your old anxiety-producing scripts and replacing them with rational scripts will not be enough. You must act on them. This doesn't mean sitting around waiting for opportunities to land in your lap. Choose plans of action and follow them. If you have no immediate goals that enable you to practise your new behaviours, then invent some silly exercises.

I often have given 'shame-attacking' exercises to clients who were afraid of their own shadows. Here are some assignments I've used. I urge you to try a few.

1. Go to work wearing one white sock and one black sock.
2. Enter sundry stores and ask for change — especially shops with signs saying, 'We don't give change'.
3. Ride a crowded elevator and call out every floor with a loud voice.
4. Ride on a bus during the rush hour and loudly call out each street.
5. On a hot day, put on a swimsuit, go to a park, and sit in the children's paddling pool.

6. Visit a feminist bookstore and ask for a book by a well known sexist.
7. Visit a nudist camp.
8. Go to an ordinary party dressed in drag.
9. Visit the most expensive clothing shop you can find while wearing the rattiest work clothes you own.
10. Go to a busy park and strike up a conversation with twenty strangers.

Okay, on the surface these exercises seem silly; nonetheless, they can be dynamite in helping you challenge wacky beliefs about self-worth. What these experiences do is give you counterevidence that challenges your old superstitions. You'll see for yourself that you can withstand disapproval countless times without becoming the incredible shrinking schmuck. Thereafter, when you tell yourself you can stand rejection by other people, it will have the ring of truth. You will have seen repeatedly that you don't grow wattles or sprout feathers if others think you're a turkey. John Dewey, the great American educator, once noted that *nothing is ever really learned until it is experienced*. This is a profound truth; so sally forth and buttress your new self-talk with actions.

As you begin to act on your new self-talk you'll find it gets easier to separate yourself from your actions. This will free you to rate your behaviour without anxiety or guilt. This, in turn, will lead to better social skills as you see that people don't like your for yourself — they like you for your behaviour.

I've often listened to clients whining, 'But, I want to be liked for myself.' Ask yourself what this could possibly mean. As you learn to separate your total self from your individual behaviours, you'll begin to see how flaky this idea is. Generally speaking, we're not liked for ourselves; we're liked for behaviours that please other people. If you foolishly demand that others like you for yourself — whatever that may mean — you're probably in for a big disappointment.

> Generally speaking, we're not liked for ourselves; we're liked for behaviours that please other people.

Think about a woman you like. Why do you like her? What emerges as you think about this question? Isn't it the way she acts when you're with her? You may even divide your friendships according to certain behaviours. You may have movie-going friends, bridge friends, hiking friends, and so forth. You like to see movies with Frank. He's a knowledgeable film buff who understands the intricacies of scripts, directing, editing, and so forth. He's fun to chat with after seeing a film. On the other hand, you never play tennis with him. He argues over your calls, loudly curses, throws his rackets, and is often morose when he loses. The truth is you don't like Frank for himself, you like him as your favourite movie-going buddy.

If you can't like Frank for himself, does that mean there is no self we can identify? Of course not. There clearly is something we call the self. There is an experiential something at the core of personhood — a something that sees, hears, and dreams; a something that thinks, feels, and becomes sexually aroused. That something will be around as long as you live; so learn to live with it. After all, you have no choice.

This brings us to some more windbaggery found in the world of psychotherapy, that sacred cow known as *self-acceptance*. Have you ever thought about what this might be? If you have, and if you're worried about not having it, forget it. Self-acceptance is a daffy goal if *self* refers to your being. The fact is you absolutely *must* accept your actual being. You can refuse to accept a package from USP, but you cannot decline to accept yourself as an existent being — which is just as well. It's one less problem to worry about.

> This brings us to some more windbaggery found in the world of psychotherapy, that sacred cow known as self-acceptance.

I suggest you let the philosophers, theologians, and psychiatrists worry over the mysteries of what the mysterious self is. Here's a simple way to view yourself. First, stop thinking of your nebulous self as some kind of a monolithic 'I'. Think of it as **i-i-i-i-i-i-i-i-i-i**...

One i is you tying your shoelaces. Another i is you looking at a sunset. Another i is you singing in the shower. Another i is you playing chess. Visualize phrases such as 'i the plumber, i the parent, i the lover, i the golfer'. This will take you away from metaphysics and anchor your thinking in objective reality.

If you conclude you're not especially skilful at parenting, only one i is being questioned, i the parent. This i is only a single skill, not your whole being or personhood. Your totality is not under the gun if one i is below average. If Jill is anxious about her parenting skills, she's probably telling herself, *I'm a bad mother*. If she would start telling herself something like, *I don't have the best of parenting skills*, she would calm her emotion-brain, soon feel more relaxed, and focus more effectively on improving her parenting.

Try saying, *I'm a bad mother* — or father, spouse, boss, friend, pet owner, and so forth. Then try saying such things as, *I'm not very good at parenting*. Notice how different this feels. When trying new skills, try saying *I have failed*. Then say *I have failed to do X six times*. Better yet, trying saying *I haven't succeeded yet in doing X*. Compare the different gut feelings you get according to the self-talk you use. Notice that *the more accurate your self-talk is, the more tempered your feelings are.*

Always bear in mind that you have countless i's, but you have only one I. Why put your whole being on the line when all that's at stake is one little i? You may foolishly feel as though you're risking your big I when you risk rejection from another person or risk a poor performance by trying something new. The reality is that you're only risking getting a grade of F for a single activity. Only in the mythical world of self-worth is your total personhood threatened with getting an F.

If you're like most people, you carry around a single-item report card in your head. When you don't succeed at something, you foolishly grade your entire self with an F. What a strange report card this is. I say strange because you don't organize it by subjects. A valid report card would list subjects such as parenting, playing chess, dating, making money, waxing the car, mowing the lawn, washing dishes, driving, doing crossword puzzles, writing letters, and so forth. The complete list, of course, would be enormous.

Do you see how absurd a one-grade report card would be? If you carry one of these in your head, trash it at once. It's bad for your emotional health. Pretend you have a new report card listing 1,000 subjects. That way you can never grade more than 1/1,000 of your behaviours at any given time.

> Do you see how absurd a one-grade report card would be?

When I do battle with my self-grading habits, I find it handy to invent epigrams and use them in my self-talk. They help condense a cluster of ideas into one pithy sentence. Here are a few samples:

1. Self-grading is **de**-grading.
2. Work at **doing** better, not **being** better.
3. **Do** what is worthwhile; don't try to **be** worthwhile.
4. Scorecards are for golf, not for people.

I'm sure you're not thrilled by these crude maxims; so dream up some of your own. If you invent your own, they'll be more meaningful to you and easier to remember. Once you've created a few, post them around your home or workplace. Repeatedly seeing them will help you chip away at your old self-worth thinking.

Compared to self-grading, grading a single performance is easy. For one thing, it's based on reality. When you go bowling, you count the number of pins you knock down and write down a score. The score is based on something solid, wooden pins scattered by a ball.

When you grade yourself, however, you enter a fanciful world of words, words, and more words — a domain that possesses little objective reality. Suppose you believe that to be incompetent is to be worthless. This leads to self-talk such as, *I am worthless because I am incompetent.* Now stop a minute and think about what 'worthless' means in actual usage. Suppose you hear somebody say *Ezra is a worthless, no-good varmint, if ever there was one. He can't do nuthin right.* We can reasonably conclude that being 'worthlesss' and being 'incompetent' are roughly the same thing — at least according to the way we hear them being used.

If this is true, we can substitute 'worthless' for 'incompetent'. Voilà! We come up with a real gem: *I'm worthless because I'm worthless.* Not very informative. You see, defining yourself as bad is purely definitional. It's a crazy word game, a fast spin around the mulberry bush. As such, it has nothing to do with the real world. Like most myths, the myth of self-worth is spun from a gleaming gossamer of ghostly threads. Created purely out of language, it never connects with the real world.

You are best served if you think of language as a road map that helps you find your way in the world. To do this, you need words that correspond to real places. If there's a city on a map, it should correspond to a real city you can reach by a road indicated on the map.

Suppose you want to find Self Worth City. You locate it on your map and follow the roads shown on the map. But suppose when you arrive, you find only a dusty field. Wouldn't you think your map was faulty? That maybe you had been cheated by the person who sold you the map?

People often buy phony maps to Self-Worth City. Some toil for years following a mapped road to this elusive Shangri-la. For example, many people spend years working toward a PhD; yet, when they finally are awarded their degree, they often have an attack of a malady known as 'post-doctoral blues'. They've toiled for years trekking down a long road and finally reached their goal, only to find they still feel worthless. They bitterly discover they've been carrying around a defective map — a linguistic maze leading nowhere.

Even with these bitter disappointments, some people won't surrender their belief in self-worth. They cling to the myth of self-worth because they think it's the basis for morality. We're taught this hokum as children. When little Johnny does good (what his mother wants), he is a 'good' little boy. If he does bad (what his mother doesn't want), he is a 'bad' little boy.

By the age of seven or eight, most of us have absorbed the belief that we achieve goodness or self-worth by winning the approval of parents, teachers, preachers, and so on. We accept the notion that if we please others and perform well, we gain approval — or what is in our minds the same thing — worthiness.

Alas, dear reader, this is a flimsy foundation to build morality on. When morality rests on a foundation of self-worth, it rests on a delicate web of diaphanous words — a flimsy support that can vanish in an instant. Of course, it can also reappear faster then the speed of light. When a parent is abusive toward a child, the parent is bad. When a parent is loving toward a child, the parent is good. Is such a parent really good one moment and bad the next? What can we say, for example, about the man who steals from his boss, but who is such a softie he takes in every stray cat in the neighbourhood? Is this man truly a bad man one moment and a good man the next? Or do we accept the obvious — that only his actions are rateable, while his personhood belongs to another category?

> Alas, dear reader, this is a flimsy foundation to build morality on.

We can certainly see that child-abuse and stealing are bad for society, but how would you prove a *person* was bad for society? We can't be hurt by somebody's personhood. We can only be hurt by a person's actions. Why not simply abandon this hopeless rating of persons and focus our attention on harmful behaviour by ourselves and others?

What's wrong with the Golden Rule as a basis for morality? Decide what kind of world you want to live in, and act accordingly. Playing the blame game only does harm to ourselves and society. Do we really need guilt to act morally? This destructive idea will not make us moral or create a more compassionate society. On the contrary, there is much evidence to suggest that guilt leads to cruel and vindictive acts toward ourselves and others.

This brings us to the issue of punishment. If you decide you are bad by reason of doing bad, you may neurotically punish yourself. You may see yourself as undeserving and deny yourself a needed vacation, or a new tennis racket, or a lobster dinner, or a new dress. You may

> This brings us to the issue of punishment.

condemn your loved ones for their inevitable mistakes and act cruelly toward them. Try to understand that punishment is nothing more than revenge — a way to vent anger or hate. Venting hate and anger on yourself or others won't help you or society.

Be sure, however, that you don't confuse the concepts of punishment and penalty. Penalties have the worthy goal of trying to reform behaviour. Punishment is a means to act out anger or vindictiveness. Suppose you don't allow yourself to watch a football game because you haven't done your daily sit-ups. This is a penalty you impose on yourself in an effort to modify your behaviour. On the other hand, suppose you don't buy that great cordless drill tool you've been lusting after because you were crabby with the kids. Now you're probably punishing yourself for being a 'bad' parent. Suppose you don't let little Sarah have her dessert because she didn't pick up her toys. You most likely are penalizing her in an effort to change a bad habit. Now suppose you give your spouse a deep-freeze treatment after an argument. You are almost certainly being punitive. You're not trying to make things better; you're trying to hurt your mate. (More on this when we take a look at the Jehovah complex.)

We sometimes punish ourselves with put-downs in our self-talk. A man who acts punitively toward his wife might regret his actions and say such things as *Look what you did, you damned fool! Man, are you stupid. What a bonehead. You don't deserve such a nice wife. You don't deserve her love and loyalty. You don't deserve...*

Ironically, this kind of self-whipping is often followed by better performance. This improvement, however, is not the result of the self-punishment. If you do poorly on a given day, you tend to naturally improve the next day. We all have an average level of performance to lean toward. After we perform poorly, we usually gravitate back toward our normal performance. This sequence has unfortunate results. Since the improvement follows on the heels of our self-whipping, we superstitiously come to believe that verbally kicking ourselves in the rear produces improvement in our performance.

This superstition is a two-sided coin, for the opposite happens when we do exceptionally well. When that happens, we often praise ourselves for doing a good job. So what happens next? You guessed it — the law of average performance takes over, and we go downhill on our next effort. This is normal. All human beings are pulled back toward their average after doing unusually well or badly.

I must interject a warning here. Sadly, sometimes the result of this conjunction of events is a superstitious refusal to take pride in our work for fear of jinxing our-

> I must interject a warning here.

selves. The old custom of knocking on wood reflects our irrational uneasiness with feeling pride over a job well done. By all means, take pride in a job well done. And if the good performances continue, rejoice over having moved your ability from one learning platform to a new level of excellence. That is a perfectly rational line of thought.

The irrational, superstitious thoughts I wish to focus on would never be generated if we refused to rate our totality and only rated our performances — a perfectly rational and constructive course to follow. It's when we put our total personhood on the line that we get ourselves in trouble.

The average person often bristles at the suggestion that praising the self is destructive. He or she wonders, *Why would it be foolish to praise one's self after doing a good job?* I urge you to think about it. If you turn in a super job and then foolishly feel you've thereby raised your self-worth a notch, what happens the next time you perform? Won't you feel anxious about losing your newly won self-worth? Remember, the next time you do X, you will naturally tend to go down in performance. How will you feel about having your newly inflated self-worth suddenly punctured like a balloon?

Do you see how you could become an emotional yo-yo at work and play? Why add this kind of stress to your life? Stick to grading your performance. This will give you plenty of satisfaction. You can still have the joy of mastery and the glow of pride over work well done.

Neither self-punishment nor self-praise will lead you to greater happiness and control over your life; so start attacking your self-rating habit at once. To do this, take notice of what you tell yourself when (1) you face rejection, and (2) you perform poorly.

To give some structure to your self-counselling, adhere to the following steps:

1. Start paying attention to your self-talk. When it isn't obvious what you're telling yourself, try some educated guessing.
2. Once you identify your self-talk, go through it word-by-word and challenge every thought. Ask yourself questions such as: *Is this true? Is it likely? Where's my proof?* Then reject those ideas that are illogical or not based on evidence.
3. Take paper and pencil and write new sentences for your self-talk. Make sure these sentences are based on evidence.
4. Force yourself to use your new scripts over and over again. Don't be mechanical. Be emphatic, dramatic, humorous.
5. Act on your new beliefs, and keep acting on them until they feel natural.

A sample script for handling mistakes

Wow, I really botched that job. Oh well, that doesn't make me a turd. It only proves I'm human. Only gods are perfect. Since I'm a fallible human being, I should make mistakes. I'll take a good close look at how I goofed, so I can learn something from my experience. If I learn something from my mistake, I'll be less likely to make the same mistake again.

The important thing is to focus on the problem — not on oneself. Only a little i is at stake, not your big *I*.

Sample script for handling rejection

I guess he's not interested in me. Oh well, that doesn't say anything about me — it only says something about his tastes. People reject other people for all sorts of strange reasons. A rejection doesn't diminish me. I'm still exactly the same person.

If I discover he doesn't like a behaviour of mine, I'll take a hard look at what I'm doing. I may decide it would be best for me to change that particular behaviour. On the other hand, I may decide he's being unacceptably demanding.

I don't like being rejected, but I'm not going to make a mountain out of a molehill. I can tolerate rejection without falling apart. I'll put it behind me and enjoy my relations with people who accept me.

If you wish, you can memorize and use these exact sentences. Better yet, rewrite them in your own words. Write your scripts on recipe cards, and carry them with you. When riding on the bus or taking a coffee break, take out a script card and work on your new self-talk. You'll need hundreds, perhaps thousands of repetitions to reprogramme yourself.

Remember that you must beware of *I can't-ism.* Your progress will come in mincing little steps, and there will be backsliding. Don't belittle this. When your self-talk fails, tell yourself, *I'm still not doing as well as I'd like to do, but that doesn't prove I can't do it. It's only by quitting that I guarantee failure. By stubbornly refusing to give in to my crazy self-talk, I'll eventually uproot it, and when I do, it will be well worth the effort.*

3

I Never Do Anything Right

❛ The picture of reality created inside our heads by the lack of consciousness of abstracting is not a 'map' of any existing 'territory'. It is a delusional world. ❜

S. I. Hayakawa

Two thousand years ago, the Stoic philosopher Epictetus said, 'It is not things that disturb us, but our view of things.' This seems so obvious it's hard to believe many people doubt it. But any other conclusion is crazy. If *things* truly upset us, we would be upset by events we're completely unaware of. Common sense tells us we must in some way be aware of an event before it can upset us. Have you thought about why people defend keeping a secret by arguing, 'What he doesn't know can't hurt him'?

If perception is essential, we are faced with an obvious question: what is it that happens when we perceive an event and get upset? What is it in the process of perception that triggers our anger? Or anxiety? Or depression? What goes wrong? Do we have a perceptual Achilles' heel? Do we — perchance — look through a glass darkly? Is our vision enigmatically flawed?

Let's start at square one — the miracle of human sight. The visual process begins when little particles of light (called photons) bounce off an object. A lens in the eye collects these scattered particles into an image, which strikes a membrane at the back of our eye. From there, the image races to the optic nerve and brain.

So far, so good — our perception has formed according to the laws of nature. Up to this point, nature is controlling our perception. We have little to say about what we see, or don't see.

But now something decisive happens. Once this image reaches our brain, we take our first step toward the creation of emotion: we evaluate what we see. We weigh, sort out, measure. Perhaps most importantly, we decide if something is good or bad for us. If we think an event is bad for us, our emotion-brain may respond with an infusion of rage, fear, or despair. This, then, is a critical moment. If we stumble at this point, if we make an irrational judgment, we pay a high price in the form of needless emotional pain.

So what are these mistakes? What do they look like? Do they number in the thousands? Are they equal to life's problems in number and complexity? Not to worry, for we are quite primitive in our repertoire of screwups. We create our emotional pain with two simple mistakes when confronted with a negative happening: (1) we grossly exaggerate the problem, or (2) we demand that it not exist.

The second of these mistakes, that of demandingness, will be tackled in Chapter 4. In this chapter, I will dissect and attack the almost universal habit of exaggerating the small and large frustrations of our daily lives.

We'll bypass many forms of exaggeration: poetic licence, amusing hyperbole, political rhetoric, puffing the product, and other colourful speech. The focus will be on something I call *horribilizing*. Some call it *catastrophizing*. Others call it *terribilizing*. Dr Albert Ellis calls it **awfulizing**. Pick your own term. What we will be interested in is the massive amount of surplus meaning behind these words.

So what about the word *horrible*? What exactly is horribleness? What does it look like? Does it have shape, weight, colour? If you were a visiting archeologist from another planet, and you were given the job of collecting samples of horribleness, how would you

So what about the word horrible?

go about finding them? Or photographing them? The fact is you could search forever and never find horribleness anywhere on the planet. Why? Because *horribleness does not exist*, at least not in the objective world. It can never be seen, touched, measured, weighed, or photographed. Horribleness has a purely subjective existence — an essence that dwells exclusively in the mind.

Those things that exist in the objective world are capable of somehow being observed — at least in theory. We can test, weigh, or measure such things to confirm their existence. But when we apply these tests to horribleness, we find we are dealing with a ghostly wisp, an evanescent shadow.

Nonetheless, we know that bad things do happen in our lives. As we vainly struggle to find a tangible form of horribleness, we do run into something negative that is starkly and objectively real. Not horribleness, mind you, but something impeding us in our quest for a good life. Alas, we also discover that our language doesn't have a word for this something; therefore, for lack of a better word, I'm going to follow the lead of Dr Albert Ellis, who labels this something *inconvenience*.

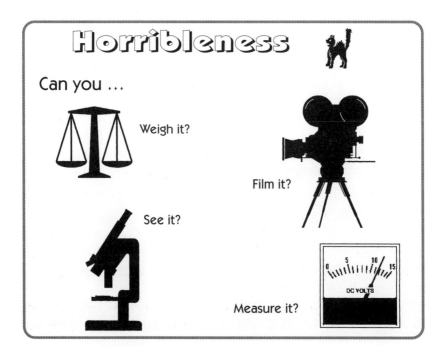

At first, this concept throws some people, but please be patient.

Contain your annoyance. If you can, suspend your sense of what the word 'inconvenience' connotes. Stay with me as we explore the objective reality behind this abstract notion.

By shifting our focus to inconvenience, we gain some clear advantages. We can readily observe it, measure it, assign numbers to it. Suppose you are stuck in a traffic jam and are delayed twenty minutes. You can measure your inconvenience and attach the number twenty. You even have an accurate tool for measurement — your watch.

Perhaps you are still bridling at my use of the word inconvenience. You are wondering how I can possibly use it to cover the whole range of life's nasty problems. After all, some of life's misfortunes are extremely painful and destructive. I totally agree. The breadth and depth of negative events in human life are indeed dramatic.

Nonetheless, a large range within a scale does not invalidate the scale. A thermometer may measure temperatures from 50 degrees below zero to 130 degrees above zero — a huge range. Does that make the thermometer invalid? Keep this analogy in mind, and bear with me as I construct an imaginary scale of inconvenience.

At one end of this imaginary scale, we will put death — the maximum inconvenience. At the other end, we can put thousands of tiny aggravations: a pimple, a hiccup, a muggy day, a rude clerk, an overcooked egg.

Now let's take a look at how our fictive scale works in an imaginary case study. Suppose you are hiking through the woods and a tick attaches itself to your leg. The removal of this tenacious little bloodsucker will take time and effort. Time and effort are measurable. In other words, we can assign numbers to your inconvenience: it takes time to remove the tick or to shop for some disinfectant. We can also measure the inflammation and swelling of the bite. We can take your temperature. And so forth.

Now let's suppose the problem gets worse. The wound gets infected. Your temperature climbs to 103 degrees. You call your doctor. She hospitalizes you

> **Now let's suppose the problem gets worse.**

for tests and observation. Notice how easily we can assign numbers to your inconvenience; the time lost from work and play,
your temperature, your blood count. And so forth. Note that being
able to assign such numbers is a sign we are dealing with objective reality.

Now let's follow the arrow moving up our imaginary scale.
Let's say the scale runs from 1 to 100, with 100 representing
death. Let's arbitrarily assign a value of 2 to the original tick bite.
Of course, now things are worse. You are sick and in the hospi-
tal. So let's move the arrow on the scale of inconvenience to
number 20.

A value of 20 is still rather low; so let's paint a grimmer sce-
nario. Suppose your infection gets worse and gangrene sets in.
Your doctor is forced to amputate your leg — certainly a dramatic
upswing on our fictive scale. We can easily observe the increase in
your inconvenience. You will need more time for many everyday
activities — more time to dress, more time to do your shopping,
more time to exercise. Then there's time spent on rehabilitation,
training, and countless adjustments. Keep in mind that we can
observe your inconvenience, and we can *measure* it with a clock.

Things definitely have got worse, so let's move the arrow on
the scale — say to 50. Alas, your problems get still worse. You
get severe blood poisoning. You are put in intensive care and
hooked up to a life-support system. At this point, we might push
the arrow up to 80. Of course, if you die, the arrow hits the gong
at the top of the scale.

Do you see how we can expand the concept of inconvenience
to cover a large range of problems that interfere with our lives? I
admit this imaginary scale has its weaknesses. We could quibble
over cases where death is preferable to life, but I don't want to
get bogged down in arguments about degrees of inconvenience.
This scale is only a gimmick invented to make a point.

By now you may be thinking Franklin is a ghoul — or at best,
some kind of macabre crackpot. How can he possibly say no
event is horrible? Please control your sense of outrage, and
remember: I'm talking about the *objective* world — the world we
can see, touch and hear. If we took an inventory of every item in

the objective world, we would not include horribleness. Horribleness is simply what we *think* about the objective world. It is something we superimpose on the world. It's a kind of filter we look through as we examine the dire events of life. Yes, horribleness does have a kind of existence — but only in the *subjective* world. That is to say, it resides exclusively in one's thoughts.

This undeniable fact makes horribleness private, idiosyncratic, and culture-bound. After all, there is no law of nature mandating how a tragedy must be viewed. If there were such a law, how would we explain the vast diversity in how people rate the same misfortunes in their lives? Why, for example, does one handicapped person deem his or her disability an unbearable burden, while another insists the same handicap is only a 'nuisance'?

These dramatic differences are hallmarks of the subjective world. We define the outside world in terms of our fears, our hopes, our habits, our expectations, our past experiences. In other words, these 'truths' are definitional. The fact is we define our own goblins into existence. We populate our objective world with an extravagant panoply of horrors — horrors that trigger our rage and desperation, horrors we could easily do without.

Who needs these monsters? Reality offers us plenty of pain and frustration. Why add more? Do we want an overlay of cryptic horror added to reality? Or do we want to see our problems as clearly as possible? Let's refocus and

> **Who needs these monsters?**

seek the kind of self-talk that will liberate us from the human propensity to see the world through a glass darkly.

Admittedly, this is easier said than done. You will need some guidance. The road to your new self-talk is marked with verbal potholes and semantic land mines. Seeking and creating self-talk is mostly a linguistic enterprise. Language, however, is a devilish thing. It often hypnotizes us into believing we're saying something about the real world when we're only describing chimeras of the imagination.

Furthermore, we tend to speak of these horrors *tautologically*. This unwieldy term is a concept from logic that means speaking in circles. We looked at a tautology in Chapter 2: 'I am worthless, because I am worthless'. This mindless circularity underlies most horribilizing.

So how do you spot circularity? And how do you know if you are merely defining something as true? There is one easy check. Look for the appearance of a word, or its equivalent, in its own definition. Let's explore an example of how this works.

So how do you spot circularity?

Take Henry. This man has a thing for nutty tautologies. I remember the day his lover Sally got furious at him and told him to get lost. Henry came to cry on my shoulder. He told me something 'terrible' had happened. He tearfully described how Sally had dumped him and how devastated he felt. I asked Henry why it was 'terrible'. Henry said, 'Well, don't you think it's an awful thing to do, dump me when I've been so loyal and giving? After all, I've invested five years in this relationship.'

Now examine carefully what Henry is saying. He's saying Sally's behaviour is 'terrible' because it's an 'awful' thing to do. As you can see, he has merely substituted *awful* for *terrible*. Since both words mean roughly the same thing, Henry is speaking and thinking in circles. He is **defining** his problem as 'terrible'. And why is it terrible? It's terrible because it's a terrible thing to do.

Not all our thought circles are so obvious. Sometimes these circles are hidden in the meaning we give to a situation. Often only a probing semantic analysis can bring them to the surface. But you can do much to avoid this linguistic quagmire if you remember one general principle: *we cannot define something into existence*. We cannot, through mere words, populate the world with the chimeras of our mind. If you believe awfulness exists in objective reality, you believe so through sheer faith.

Sure, it does sound as though you're talking about the real world when you talk about the 'terrible' thing your lover did. After all, they clearly did some kind of *thing*. But the terribleness of that something does not reside in the thing — it resides in your head. When you characterize what your lover did as 'terrible', you are also reporting something in your head — your feelings about your lover's behaviour. You unwittingly talk as though something ghostly were something corporeal. But the truth is you are not simply reporting an objective fact, you are reshaping the facts with distortional subjectivity.

In order to manage these stirred-up emotions through rational self-talk, you must be able to separate your opinion of an event from the event itself. Consider the following pairs of statements:

Jane is a bad student.	Jane got two Fs.
Johnny is a brat.	Johnny kicked my cat.
AIDS is ghastly.	AIDS kills millions.
Helen acted coldly.	Helen didn't hug me.
This is a great car.	This car always starts.

Imagine using a video camera to film each of these items. You would have no problem filming the second column of events, but how would your camera record the first column?

Dr Maxie Maultsby makes this question a key part of psychotherapy. He asks his clients to imagine *exactly* what sights and sounds a video camera would record. He calls this the 'camera check'. This can be a terrific tool in your self-help kit. If you discipline yourself to use the camera check consistently, you can greatly sharpen your reality perceptions. Use it with unflinching honesty, and you will soon learn that words such as *bad*, *brat*, *horrible*, *cold*, *great*, and so forth, reflect your evaluations, not objective reality.

If I were to visit my friend Helen, and she didn't hug me, a videotape could easily record this. It could not, however, record her 'coldness'. For you see, *coldness* (in this sense) does not exist in the empirical world — the world of shoes and ships and sealing wax. Neither I nor the camera can see Helen's coldness. I can only opine she is acting coldly, and this opinion is not the same as a fact of the world. The coldness of Helen's behaviour is not a *thing* found among the furniture of the world; it is simply my subjective view of her behaviour.

So be extremely wary; for many thoughts that seem like facts are merely opinions. You may protest and say, 'But a thought is *something*. Surely we can't say a thought is nothing.' I agree; thoughts undeniably exist. Your having a thought is a fact — a somewhat peculiar fact that is accessible only to you, but still a fact. If I think Johnny is a little brat, my thought is an opinion, but it also is a fact that I've had the thought.

This means that when you use the camera check to recall events as clearly as possible, you may justifiably include a foot-note saying you had a specific thought at the time of the event. Be careful, though. Treat your thought as an editorial footnote. Focus primarily on what your imaginary camera would have recorded. Only then should you examine the thought you had at the time.

Scrutinize the thought carefully. Ask yourself a battery of questions such as: 'Does my thought correspond precisely with what my camera would have filmed? Does my thought have an evidential basis? Is it logical? How do I know it's true? Where's my proof? Am I sounding a false alarm, an apprehension based on the whimsies of my imagination?'

Remember that Dummibrain is a sucker for phony alarms. If you exag-gerate your problems with overblown self-talk, he'll see a simple frustration as an imminent danger and instinc-tively pull your panic lever. Stubbornly resist the temptation to add a subjective overlay to your problems. Try to evaluate your problems in a cut-and-dried manner. The more objective you are, the less overwrought Dummibrain will become. This inverse ratio is a consistent feature of human nature.

> Remember that Dummibrain is a sucker for phony alarms.

Now that we have explored this quintessentially human trait, we are ready to take a look at the title for this chapter: *I Never Do Anything Right*. Have you ever said this to yourself after a blun-der? Chances are you've said something similar from time to time. And how many times have you heard others say this? More importantly, do you see how crazy this thought is? Think about it. If you actually never did anything right, you wouldn't survive one day in modern society. The first time you crossed a street, you wouldn't wait for a break in traffic; you'd wait for a speeding truck and step into its path. You wouldn't have a cup of coffee for breakfast; you'd pour yourself a cup of insecticide. And so forth.

To see how crazy this kind of self-talk is, imagine making a list of all the things you do in a day. The list would be astronomical: walking, sitting, standing, eating, drinking, dressing, talking, opening doors, using a fork, and so forth. These, and thousands of other small acts, are all things you do — and do correctly. The number of mistakes you make on your worst day is certain to be minuscule.

Let's say that one day you make ten blunders — a lousy day by anyone's standards. Furthermore, let's say you do 10,000 things correctly. This generates a fraction of 10/10,000. Put another way, your goofs comprise 1/10 of 1% of what you do on a bad day. You can see how the assertion *I never do anything right* is daffy from a statistical viewpoint.

This statistical blindness is evident in other self-talk phrases. 'Everything went wrong today. Nothing is going right today. Nothing ever goes right for me. I just can't seem to do anything right.' Ironically, this talk often is based on two or three mistakes. 'So what's the big deal?' you ask. 'This exaggeration seems harmless. So what if we sometimes get exasperated and stretch the facts a little?'

The problem is Dummibrain. He has big ears and is forever eavesdropping on your self-talk. Your thinking brain knows perfectly well not everything went wrong at the office. But your emotion-brain only hears what you literally say to yourself. To your old brain, your self-talk may sound like an eyewitness account of Armageddon.

> The problem is Dummibrain.

If you want to avoid getting Dummibrain in a panic, learn to use your camera check. It's one of the best tools you have for curtailing your urge to exaggerate. Here's a simple example of how it works. Suppose Henry decides to visit Sally on a Thursday night. When he drops by her house, Sally tells him she's had a hard day, she's tired, and she'd like to spend the evening alone.

A disappointed Henry tells Sally he understands and leaves. Then he goes home and broods. He broods until he's in a deep depression. His self-talk goes like this: 'I guess Sally thinks I'm boring. I can see it in her eyes — she doesn't love me anymore! I guess this is the end for us. God, how awful. I don't see how I can get along without her. I feel torn apart. I can't stand this pain.'

Now let's suppose Henry knows how to use camera checks. Instead of brooding and depressing himself, suppose he imagines what a video camera would have recorded during his visit. What a pleasant surprise! Using this form of objective replay, he doesn't hear Sally say words such as, 'I don't love you anymore. You bore me. I don't like your company.' With a good mental videotape, Henry would see Sally saying she's dog-tired and needs some time to recover from a lousy day. The tape would show her smiling and affectionately touching Henry on the cheek — a scene far less ominous than the one pictured by Henry's initially overblown self-talk.

Extreme magnifications of reality often intertwine with another bad habit. Many quarrels (if not a majority) result from not listening to what others are saying. You see, there's a difference between listening and hearing. When Sally says something to Henry, he hears her, but he also instantly evaluates what she says. In the process, he exaggerates or adds to what she says. He may even block out crucial parts of what she says. This is poor listening. The ear hears, but the mind doesn't listen.

To make matters worse, people such as Henry often fail to express their dotty ideas to their partners. Henry says something to himself and then mentally answers himself. And so forth. Instead of having a dialogue with Sally, he has a conversation with himself. This does little to straighten out his distorted perceptions.

To see how this works, let's envision a short scene with the two lovers. Henry is late for his date with Sally. Sally asks him why he's late. Henry hears her words and instantly evaluates what she's saying. At this point, two of Henry's bad habits come

Henry is getting mad — but not over Sally's words;
he's making himself angry with his own self-talk.

into play: (1) he automatically magnifies what he hears, and (2) he adds an overlay of irrational condemning.

Let's first consider what Sally actually says: 'Why are you late, honey? I was worried sick.' These spoken words belong to objective reality. We can record them with a video camera. Compare this reality with what is going on in Henry's subjective world. Note his use of absolutes. He thinks, 'Why is she bugging me? Nag, nag, nag. She's *always* nagging me. She *never* lets up on me. She's *constantly* trying to put me down.'

Henry, of course, thinks Sally is being a real shrew. He explodes and says, 'Can't you ever let up on me? Always nagging. Always putting me down. I can't help it if I was late. You're always bitching.'

Poor Sally, she's dumbfounded. She thinks Henry is responding to her innocent question. She thinks she's having a normal conversation with Henry. Not so. He isn't actually answering her words. What Sally doesn't know is that Henry is responding to his own thoughts. It never occurs to her that Henry is, in a sense, talking to himself. And not only is he carrying on a private conversation inside his head — he's getting angry over what he's hearing himself say.

Bizarre, you say? Maybe, but this peculiar ritual is common among neurotics. Henry's anger, of course, is related to his exaggerations — *always, never, constantly*. This absolutist language clutters the self-talk of screwballs like Henry.

Here are the most commonly used exaggerations: *always, never, every, none, everything, nothing, everybody, nobody*. Watch out for these words. They can be dangerous to your emotional serenity.

Like most people, you probably need some linguistic housecleaning. If you're in the least bit typical, you almost certainly use self-talk littered with verbal magnifiers. Find them, attack them, replace them. You don't have to tackle them all at once. Start with one word: the adverb *always*. Carry a small notebook for a week and record every instance of always in your speech or thoughts.

As you sensitize yourself to how often you use this word, begin questioning each usage. If you tell yourself such things as, 'I always forget my chequebook', challenge your exaggeration. Try saying the same sentence with *sometimes*, or *occasionally*, or *once in a while*. Use exact numbers whenever possible. Get in the habit of using terms such as *once, twice, three times*. Use terms that demagnify — words such as *seldom, rarely, hardly ever*. Be playfully creative with your new vocabulary. Do it in a way that suits you. But *do* it. Set a goal of reducing your use of the word always by 75%. Then go on to the next item in your inventory of overblown adjectives and adverbs.

Do this systematically, and you'll soon start to feel calmer. You don't have to take my word for it. Work for several weeks at cleaning out words such as *always*. You'll be amazed at how fast you begin to feel better.

> **Do this systematically, and you'll soon start to feel calmer.**

Censoring your vocabulary is relatively simple. All you need is a little vigilance and a list of targeted words. A word of caution: not all your script rewriting will be this simple. Not all exaggerated language is easily detected or uprooted. Often words are only implied or are buried in code language. Take simple statements such as 'Life is unfair', or 'Life is a bitch'. When Henry mindlessly parrots these sentences, he irrationally implies that *all* of life is unfair or nasty.

You will have to do some digging to uncover these hidden absolutes. Sentences are often elliptical, leaving out words that are understood. Try to infer what is unspoken; then replace these hidden absolutes with more accurate words. This will help you to get a better handle on what you actually are saying or thinking. Take the declaration, 'Life is unfair'. If you spot this in your self-talk, and you suspect the sentence is elliptical, try substituting another sentence — one that states your probable meaning. In this case, you might discover that your real meaning is, '*All* of life is *always* unfair'.

The next step is to replace your exaggeration with an honest statement. In other words, you will replace a falsehood with a truth. In this case, you might try something like *Yes, people sometimes act unfairly, but we're all fallible human beings. Most of the time people act fairly.* Or you could try something like *It's true life sometimes plays dirty tricks, but it's also true life sometimes gives us wonderful surprises.* This is merely being more realistic. (Not to be confused with positive thinking, which is neither realistic nor believable.)

We hide exaggerations in our self-talk in various ways. The use of red herrings is common. Good therapists quickly spot these diversionary tactics. A client may show up for a session in a state of emotional upheaval. When asked what the problem is, the client may say something like *My boss didn't like a report I wrote.* A rational therapist will instantly be suspicious. She knows a thought like this one is unlikely to push her client into a huge funk. In short, the client probably is not tuned into the true causes of her bad feelings.

> We hide exaggerations in our self-talk in various ways.

In order to probe beneath the client's initial explanation, I may use a *so-what* technique. This consists of repeatedly asking,

'So what?' Regardless of what the client says regarding the 'catastrophe' in his or her life, I always reply with 'So what?' A session with my client Mournful Morrie might sound like this:

Franklin: *Okay, tell me about your big catastrophe.*
Morrie: *My boss rejected my report.*
Franklin: *So what?*
Morrie: *He said it was a bad report.*
Franklin: *So what?*
Morrie: *Maybe he thinks I didn't work hard enough.*
Franklin: *So what?*
Morrie: *I feel like he's putting me down.*
Franklin: *So what?*
Morrie: *That makes me feel small.*

At this point I might jump in and say, 'Now we're getting somewhere. That kind of message can easily worry Dummibrain. From his naïve perspective, being turned into the incredible shrinking man is no small matter. No wonder you feel anxious.

'To avoid these destructive feelings, it's important to listen carefully to why your boss didn't like your report. It's definitely in your best interest to graciously redo it, but as you do so, be sure to stay focused on the report — not on your supposedly shrinking self-worth. A criticism of your report is not a criticism of your whole personhood. Keep your eye on the ball.'

You might want to try using the *So what?* technique in your self-talk to hammer away at your thoughts until you've reached the bedrock thought triggering your emotional turmoil, the exaggerated thought that is actually disturbing Dummibrain.

Dotty thoughts can be camouflaged in other ways. They can, for example, lie hidden in half-sentences. I can often guess what the missing half is. If a depressed client says, 'My boyfriend

> **Dotty thoughts can be camouflaged in other ways.**

stood me up ...' I usually can guess the unspoken part of the sentence. In this example, the invisible words might be *...and it's horrible* or *...and I can't stand it.*

As you practise deducing the missing parts of your half-sentences, you will find that the kind of emotion you feel is a clue to the missing half-sentence. Anxiety, for example, may stem from a half-sentence such as *...and I feel put down.* By the end of this book you will begin to see these links. Once you master this deductive backtracking, you will begin to make sense out of why you 'overreact' to events.

You see, people don't actually overreact to events; they are reacting to overblown self-talk; so in a sense, they're not really overreacting. Such inflated self-talk, if believed by the old brain, would upset anybody. So if you think you're 'overreacting' to something, start digging. And keep digging until you find a thought that can sensibly account for the intensity of your feelings.

To do this, you can use a fill-in-the-blank method. It goes like this: Your lover does something you don't like, and you get upset. Your reaction, however, is way out of proportion to the event. You realize you had best search for a hidden thought; so you take a paper and pencil and write a heading like this: *Mary didn't pay any attention to me at the party last night, and* _____.

Then you make a list of thoughts to be tested in the blank space. For example, *I was bored, I felt ignored, I didn't like the way she was flirting with Jim,* and so forth. Keep trying different fill-ins, no matter how silly they may seem. Use free association, and go with the unfettered flow of your thoughts.

How will you know when you've plugged in the thought that is actually upsetting you? That's not easy to answer. This method is more art than science. I find that when I plug in the responsible thought, a bell goes off in my head. I have what the psychologists call an 'Aha!' reaction, and I know at once that I've collared the culprit thought.

A word of warning about this method. If you worry obsessively about your mythical self-worth, you may resist recognizing the screwy ideas floating in your stream of consciousness. Try to relax, and remind yourself that all human beings have irrational thoughts. Join the human race, and admit to having a substantial amount of dotty thinking. We're all fallible, and we all have thoughts that are distinctly odd.

This fear of admitting one has nutty thoughts probably underlies the use of gimmicks such as half-sentences. Mind you, I don't mean to imply that all such ellipses are hiding screwy thinking. Speaking in half-sentences often cloaks irrational thoughts, but not always. Some elliptical language can be useful.

Suppose I say, 'All American stop signs are octagonal.' When I use the absolute *all*, I'm merely leaving out the restrictive clause, *all those I've ever seen*. Often the words *all* and *none* are abbreviations for *almost all* and *almost none*. I don't want you to neurotically worry about every casual use of figurative or elliptical language when you're problem solving. I'm only saying you should avoid sloppy language when you're problem solving. Ordinary language is far too imprecise to be used in rational self-counselling.

Sensing that most irrational language is vague, we devise other tricks in addition to half-sentences. We often try to make our exaggerations sound more precise by attaching numbers. It sounds more scientific when we append numbers or percentages to our fanciful views of reality.

> Sensing that most irrational language is vague, we devise other tricks in addition to half-sentences.

I once had a client who kept insisting 90% of her problems were due to being overweight. Actually, not one of her problems was due to her weight. Another woman insisted three-fourths of all the good men were married, and the remaining one-fourth already had lovers. A depressed young man told me, 'I mess up horribly every other time I use the copy machine at work.'

These numbers and percentages seem to give respectability to our exaggerations by making them sound more solid. Numbers, after all, are tools we use to measure objective reality. Beware of these phony numbers. Don't let yourself get away with statistical mumbo-jumbo.

Voodoo numbers, coded numbers, metaphors, hyperboles, shorthands, missing words — these and other hallmarks of ordinary language make the overhauling of self-talk a tough job. You had best accept the fact that cleaning up this mess will not happen overnight. It will take time, effort, and stubborn vigilance.

Now for some good news. I've stressed to you that much of your old self-talk is hidden, well-practised, and hard to uproot; nonetheless, your new scripts will have one huge advantage — they will have logic and evidence on their side. This means they'll have a more powerful believability. Think about what a plus this is. Your new self-talk will be decisively more believable than your old self-talk.

When you get down to brass tacks, most neurotic scripts are impossible to believe except through sheer faith. In fact, most of them are simply preposterous. So take heart; logic, evidence and objective reality are powerful allies. Be happy they're on your side. You'll use these pillars to solidly support your new scripts — clusters of thought that will be far easier to accept than your old nonsense.

Another advantage rational thinking has over loony self-talk is that it enhances personal growth. Irrational self-talk is stultifying and constrictive to growth. Overgeneralizing, for example, leads to a thousand prejudices — intolerance of blacks, Jews, atheists, gays, foreigners, ethnic foods, opera, jazz, foreign films, and so on. The list is endless. People close themselves off from a vast diversity of human experience by generalizing on the basis of one or two experiences. Sometimes this closed-mindedness rests on no personal knowledge whatsoever.

A militant feminist, for example, may hate half the human race due to a few bad experiences with men. She nourishes her bigotry with dogmas such as, *Men are insensitive, manipulative, exploitative.* These exaggerations fuel her anger and lead to the belief (often hidden) that men should be punished. She may then act punitively toward any sensitive and caring man she meets. She closes the door on any chance for a happy relationship with her off-putting anger.

To avoid this trip, *proportion your beliefs to the evidence for them.* If you are using a sample of seven out of a million, your evidence is hardly overwhelming.

> To avoid this trip, proportion your beliefs to the evidence for them.

Picture it as 7/1,000,000. When we visualize our judgments this way, we see how foolish they are. Suppose I'm in the habit of saying to myself 'All women are crazy'. If I were to consider all the women I've met, in one capacity or another, the ratio between sane and nutty women I've met would be rather telling. Let's say I've met three women who are schizophrenic, and I've met 1,000 women who are not. The ratio is three to 1,000. If I make sweeping generalizations on the basis of such flimsy evidence, I'm the crazy one — not the entire female sex.

Bear in mind that if I think in such overstated ways, I'm hurting myself most of all. Prejudice is harmful to others in society, but it also erodes your own mental health; for if you overgeneralize about other people, you will also lean toward overgeneralizing about yourself. That is to say, you can easily become prejudiced toward yourself! You may, on the basis of a few mistakes, condemn your entire personhood. Self-prejudice uses the same mechanism as other-prejudice. And, just as you may punish others, you may punish yourself for being unworthy or bad.

This self-prejudice is a product of overgeneralizing, but it isn't the only result. Irrationally magnified judgments lead to a closed-mindedness that radically limits one's ability to learn. Take the example of Henry, who accused Sally of being a nag. Sally naturally denies Henry's unfounded charges, but Henry has a closed mind. She denies, he insists. The argument accelerates. Words fly.

As the spat heats up, Henry is more sure than ever he's right. He focuses entirely on defending his neurotic exaggerations about Sally's 'nagging'. He has closed his mind to any counter-evidence. In short, his dogmatism is strangling his ability to negotiate, to learn, and to grow.

This brings us to what I call the *vested-interest fallacy*. Henry has built a vested interest in his claim. This interest is more than a simple desire to be right. Henry, who believes in the myth of self-worth, has put his value as a person on the line. His interest in proving himself right is actually an interest in preserving his self-worth. To this end, he frantically defends his claims.

This brings us to what I call the vested-interest fallacy.

The intellectual fallacy he commits is his suppression of any evidence counting against his belief. Consciously, or unconsciously, he rejects any evidence Sally offers. As he gets more anxious, he refuses to admit even one counter instance. If Sally points out the many times she has been patient about Henry's tardiness, Henry is sure to pooh-pooh her examples.

This discounting of everything Sally says rests on a common human foible. Henry, like most people, treats his opinions as facts, while treating the opinions of others as just that — opinions. He repeatedly tells Sally, 'That's just your opinion.' His attitude is all too clear — what Henry says is fact; what Sally says is opinion.

Few souls are so brash as to say this, but a little observation will tell you many people secretly think this way. You would do well to assume this delusion colours your own attitudes. To ferret out this pomposity, pay attention to how you behave in arguments. Do you **act** as though your claims were facts, while the other person's assertions are merely opinions?

Another way to track down the vested-interest fallacy in your own thinking is to take a good look at your most cherished beliefs. You probably keep a lookout for new facts that support a pet theory. But how often do you collect evidence counting against your belief? Your heart may leap with glee whenever you come across something that buttresses a favourite thesis. But do you deftly close your eyes and ears to any new information that challenges your thesis?

If this sounds familiar, you had best make a vigorous effort to change your ways. Start reminding yourself that you won't magically shrink if one of your strongly held opinions is refuted. Keep reminding yourself that your opinion is exactly that — an opinion. Tell yourself this no matter how ardently you embrace a theory. Mathematics can offer certainty, but all our other beliefs are based purely on probabilities. It may be a humbling experience to do so, but accepting this truth will make you a stronger person.

Opening your mind in this way will help you rewrite your scripts. As you open up to the possibility that you hold some mistaken beliefs, you will be better prepared to trash the nonsense you find in your self-talk. You may, for example, be more accepting of the possibility that you have a negative view of yourself.

The importance of this can hardly be exaggerated. If you have such a view, it can lead to depression. Depression, in turn, tends to further close your mind about who and what you are. When depressed, you may develop highly exaggerated prejudices toward yourself — views you stubbornly cling to despite much counter evidence.

> The importance of this can hardly be exaggerated.

Dr Aaron Beck has deeply studied the links between depression and exaggeration. He describes depression as resting on three clusters of beliefs. He calls them the *cognitive triad of depression*. Beck found that depressed people have exaggerated negative views about: (1) themselves, (2) the world around them, and (3) their future prospects.

Ellis, Beck, and others have found that depressed people consistently have overblown thoughts such as: *I'm a born loser. I'm hopelessly incompetent. I'm totally useless. I'm no good to anybody.*

Have you ever had thoughts like these? Have you heard others say these things? How would you rewrite these sentences so as to make them more rational? Take a few minutes to write down some rational alternatives. Make sure you give special attention to the absolutes. Pick an alternative word, and start using it in your self-talk.

As you can see, depressed people distort the world they live in. Their thinking and self-talk are riddled with exaggerations. Typical whoppers are: *I have nothing but bad luck. I never get any breaks. My boss never appreciates anything I do. My neighbours are always giving me grief. The people I work with are absolutely unbearable. My kids are completely irresponsible. My mother is driving me crazy. My life is nothing but a pile of dung.*

How would you rewrite these depression-generating sentences? Try formulating some reality-based thoughts. Keep in mind that when I say 'reality-based', I'm recognizing that there may be a seed of truth underlying some of these statements. The trick is not to deny actual negative situations, but to evaluate them without gross exaggeration.

Besides seeing their world through a glass darkly, depressed people tend to see their future as hopelessly grim. They often *neverize*. Typical thoughts are: *I'll never get anywhere. I'll never have anything. I'll never meet the right person. I'll never have a good job. I'll never get married.* How would you rewrite these sentences and eliminate the neverizing? Can you think of some alternatives to take the place of *I'll never...?*

Do you see how these thought clusters fit into the three areas of the triad of depression? Make use of Beck's paradigm. You only need to remember the three my's: (1) myself, (2) my world, (3) my future. Look for a negative thought in each area. This will give focus and structure to your self-counselling and make it seem less daunting. Having a map to follow will help you see where you're at and where you're going. As you know, every little task seems ponderously difficult when you're depressed. A scheme that organizes and directs one's self-counselling is especially helpful when you feel dispirited and listless.

When you feel drained of energy, pick the simplest self-counselling task you can think of. You might, for example, rewrite one screwy thought. Suppose you have the thought, *My boss is always riding me.* Even though you may perform the task mechanically, force yourself to write a challenge to this particular exaggeration. Suppose you answer with, *My boss doesn't ride me. I'm not a horse.* This refutes the exaggeration hidden in the dead metaphor 'riding'. This rebuttal may seem silly to you, but remember that Dummibrain is childishly naïve about language.

Simple as this one task may seem, the act of rewriting a single nutty thought is a good beginning. When depression saps your energy, you may feel weak and unable to act. A single, simple action aimed at attacking your depression creates evidence you're not a helpless pawn in the grip of irresistible forces. This, in turn, can start a snowball effect. As you inch forward, you build momentum. Try this simple motto to prod yourself forward and remind yourself you're in charge: *If I have the power to make mountains out of molehills, I have the power to unmake those same mountains.*

Mountains, of course, aren't the best metaphors for our overstated horribilizing. Mountains imply permanence. The fact is you can shrink these mountains. Ironically, one good way to fight your overblown images is to further exaggerate them. This is the technique of verbal caricature. A caricature, as you know, is an exaggeration of reality for the purpose of humour. In other words, I'm suggesting you exaggerate your exaggerations. By doing so, you will see more clearly which features of a problem you're distorting. Better yet, you may even learn to smile at some of your foibles and follies.

To illustrate, let's use this technique with Henry, our quintessential horribilizer. After Sally got mad at him, Henry was talking as though it were the end of the world. Suppose I decided to help Henry see how absurd his horribilizing was by painting a caricature of his whining. Suppose I were to say to him *What a bummer, Henry. I know how much you depended on Sally's love. For you, losing her love is like being deprived of food and water. How will you make it without her? It has to be scary for you. Your pain must be almost unbearable. I can understand why you feel life isn't worth living. How will you face life without Sally? After all, she was everything to you. Look, Henry, if you want to bail out, I'll help you. What the heck, what's a friend for? Let's see, how should we do it? A gun? Poison? Hanging? I know! I'll accidentally run over you with my car. You lie down in my driveway, and I'll back over you.*

Using this technique on another person, however, is tricky. You might get punched in the nose. It's safest and most effective when used in your own self-counselling. Learning to poke fun at your own whining is a big step forward. Humour is a powerful tool for defusing exaggerations. To energize your humour, give yourself free rein when doing self-caricatures. Let your imagination run wild. Compare your woes to a nuclear holocaust, to the global AIDS plague, to World War II.

I've often used this method when leading support groups. I ask each person to come up with the most horrible event his or her imagination is capable of conceiving. Then I list each horror on the blackboard. Once I have a list of at least a half-dozen hair-raising horrors, I quietly add a group member's personal problem to the bottom of the list.

Let's imagine using this technique with Henry. Let's suppose I ask him to list five of the greatest catastrophes he can imagine. Henry generally has a rather bleak view of the world, so he quickly comes up with a rather grim inventory of imaginary horrors. To these five I append his current problem with Sally. Let's say the final gruesome list looks like this:

Henry's catastrophe list

1. Astronauts return from space carrying a deadly virus, and all mankind dies a slow, agonizing death.
2. All life on the planet is destroyed by a nuclear holocaust.
3. I'm in a car accident, and I survive as a blind, deaf, mute quadruple-amputee.
4. I'm captured by psychotic terrorists who torture me continuously for months until I die of shock and pain.
5. A huge asteroid hits the Earth, knocking it off course, and sending it hurtling into the sun.
6. Sally is mad at me.

Henry's
catastrophe list

Some therapists call this tool *paradoxical intention*, a term coined by Victor Frankl. I call it *preposterizing*. The idea is to show how nutty one's exaggeration is, thus putting it in perspective. I suggest doing your preposterizing with impassioned histrionics. Ham it up. Wail, moan, tear your hair, lie on the floor flailing your arms and legs. I predict you'll end up with a smile or even the giggles. Keep whining about your 'catastrophe' while allowing yourself to smile. You can do this, so give it a try. Put on a smile, and start griping about some problem. Keep this up. Grin and gripe, smile and whine. Most people can't do this for long without laughing. Can you? I'll bet you can't.

So much for the use of humour. Now I want to take a look at something grim: suicide. In some groups, the number of suicides is alarming. Dentists, police, and teenagers, kill themselves with higher than average frequency. Why? Regarding teenagers, I suspect one cause is their tendency toward exaggerated self-talk. Their youth and inexperience probably play a role in their tendency to overstate run-of-the-mill problems. Mind you, I can't prove this, but I strongly suspect it.

Many of us have suicidal thoughts at one time or another, and not only during our teenage years. These thoughts are often closely linked to belief in the myth of self-worth, but simple exaggeration also plays a role. The magnification of problems can become bizarre if one has no idea how to rationally measure life's hassles.

> Many of us have suicidal thoughts at one time or another.

Several years ago, newspapers in Minneapolis reported that a teenager had hurled himself from a high bridge over the Mississippi River. He left a suicide note saying he had decided to kill himself because his favourite TV show had been cancelled.

That may seem incredible to most people, but rational therapists understand this kind of bizarre thinking. They know how easy it is for some people to steadily escalate the smallest frustration into a horror. This runaway magnifying of problems is a kind of talent people learn while children and dutifully maintain as they grow into adulthood. Like most skills, this one is kept proficient through practice.

Along with a growing fascination with suicide, many teenagers are drawn to certain dangerous drugs. This is understandable. Being prone to exaggerated views of life's hassles, teenagers often are battered by emotional storms they unleash within themselves. Not knowing how to rationally change their bad feelings, they choose to change them chemically. They learn that certain risky drugs can temporarily numb bad feelings. Of course, suicide permanently obliterates their bad feelings.

Both ways of dealing with bad feelings stem from a sense of impotence, a belief we're helpless to expunge emotional pain, a stark dread that we have no control over our emotional destinies. How sad that so many people accept this false view. In this case, ignorance is not bliss; it's a road to emotional pain, perilous drug addictions, and sometimes even death.

Ignorance of rational ways to alleviate one's emotional pain is not the only handicap we find among depressed and suicidal people. These lost souls often do not even realize what their problem is. They mistakenly think a negative event is the problem. Yet, most of the time, their main problem is that they feel bad. Don't get me wrong. I'm not saying these people don't have vexatious problems to deal with in their lives. What I'm saying is that a person considers suicide mostly because he feels bad, not because something bad has happened in his life.

Suicidal clients often are exasperated by my 'insensitivity' when I suggest they're mistaken about the cause of their depression. I usually coax them into seeing their confusion by asking, 'If you were completely happy, would you still want to kill yourself?' They usually answer, 'Why no, of course not. Why would I want to kill myself if I were happy?'

Having won this admission, I say something like, 'You see, your problem is not that your spouse has been unfaithful, *your problem is how bad you feel*. Furthermore, your extreme anger and depression are the result of focusing on your spouse's behaviour rather than your view of that behaviour.'

I then go on to say, 'If you think about this, you will find reason for some optimism. Of course, you can't change the fact your spouse has cheated on you. You can, however, modify your bad feelings. That's not to say you can make yourself feel happy about what has happened. You can't realistically feel happy about negative events; but you can reduce your anguish and depression to simple sadness — an emotion that won't cripple your life or lead you to suicide.'

Mary, a clearly depressed client, resisted this claim. She adamantly refused to admit she could change her feelings. She clung fiercely to the idea that only death could end her agony. I agreed with Mary that death would end her suffering. I said, 'I have to agree with you — death would end your pain; nonetheless, let's set that solution aside for the moment. After all, you'll always have suicide as an option. First let's look at some other options. Surely death isn't the only way a person can ease bad feelings. I tell you what, let's make a list of actions, including suicide, that you might experiment with. Just for the heck of it, let's see if we can come up with a list of ten.'

The whole point of the exercise inheres in this question: *Where does one place suicide on the list?* I ask the client to decide. After a moment's reflection, a client realizes suicide must be put last. If placed in position three, it would obliterate options four to ten. If an especially distraught client resists the obvious and wants to put suicide in fourth place, I prod him or her by saying something like, *Gee, what if number five is* **the** *method that works for you? Suppose number five is a system that would enable you to overcome your depression and live a relatively happy life?*

Obviously, survival must come first. If you're alive, and able to think, you can work toward changing your destructive irrationality. New Age nonsense would have us believe rationality constricts emotional growth. Poppycock. The abandonment of reason can be a dire threat to one's emotional health and even one's survival. Wherever and whenever you run into New Age's flowery irrationalism, stubbornly resist it. Reason has always been humankind's best tool for survival and happiness.

So as not to leave you without a road map, I offer the following guidelines for ferreting out harmful exaggerations in your self-talk.

If you feel depressed, look for these kinds of exaggerations:

1. How awful that this happened to me. Life is horribly unfair.

2. I never do anything right. I always screw up.

3. I'll never have a happy life. Nothing will ever work out for me.

If you feel anxious, look for these kinds of exaggerations:

1. What if X happens? How horrible. I couldn't stand it.

2. I can't deal with this. This is killing me.

3. Everything is falling apart in my life.

If you feel angry, look for these kinds of exaggerations:

1. What X did to me was unspeakably horrible.

2. X must be the most ungrateful and vile person alive.

3. X always does that. X never shows me any consideration.

Go over these sentences and underline all the words that are exaggerations. Replace them with more accurate terms. Build simple, accurate sentences that won't confuse or upset Dummibrain. Do you see which thoughts would be especially alarming to Dummibrain?

I've used this chapter to demonstrate that exaggeration is the most basic mistake we make when confronted with the countless hassles life thrusts upon us. Now we'll look at what is possibly the most destructive mistake of all in human thinking — *demandingness*.

4

The Jehovah Complex

6 The scientific method is concerned with how things
do happen, not how they **ought** to happen.
Knowledge of the way things do happen, with no ifs,
ands, or buts, allows us to deal more effectively with
our environment. 9

Stuart Chase

There are two ways to look at the world, two ways to organize
reality, two ways to account for events. One view sees the
world as filled with myth and magic, a domain sometimes governed by randomness and accident. The other view sees reality
as filled with energy and matter, a domain consistently governed
by cause and effect. The magical view of life postulates mythical
creatures such as self-worth and horribleness. The scientific
view of life gives us a picture of fallible human beings coping
with real frustrations.

We've used a scientific view to dismantle two superstitions:
self-worth and horribleness. Now I want to assault the most stubborn, the most destructive, the most hidden of our superstitions.
This common sorcery goes by many names: the Jehovah complex, should-ing, musturbation, grandiosity, demandingness,
and so forth. Essentially, it is a command that reality be different
from what it is. It is an insistence that the laws of the universe be
suspended to accommodate our personal whims. It is a mandate
that the sun shine when we go on a picnic, that traffic jams

vanish when we are in a hurry, that hard tasks be easy when we are struggling. It decrees that liars not lie, that murderers not murder, that the insane be sane.

These shoulds, oughts and musts are the hallmarks of thinking that rejects reality — a rejection that underlies nearly all emotional distress. A rational acceptance of reality means the difference between rage and annoyance, between despair and sadness, between panic and concern. Your emotional well-being requires that you understand one simple scientific fact: *everything is as it should be.* To reject this truth is to condemn yourself to a life of emotional storms and eruptions of destructive behaviour.

When I categorically insist that everything is as it should be, you may be outraged. Okay, be a doubting Thomas, but before you rise up in high dudgeon, hear me out. Be patient, for it takes time to get a handle on this concept. Stay with me, and you will see that both logic and evidence are on my side. Even if what I am saying sounds outlandish at this moment, restrain your annoyance until you've heard my arguments. If you hang in there, it's entirely possible you'll be rewarded with the most dazzling and important insight of your life. Pompous words? Let's see if I can back them up.

The *should* I am using is the should of science. This is the should of cause and effect, the should that gives order to the universe and makes scientific investigation possible. At bottom, science is an enterprise dedicated to uncovering shoulds embedded in the structure of the world.

When, as legend would have us believe, Galileo dropped varying sizes of cannon balls from the Leaning Tower of Pisa, he was trying to show that a difference in weight *should not* affect velocity. When Benjamin Franklin laid a black sheet and a white sheet over two patches of snow, he was trying to show that the snow under the black sheet *should* melt more quickly.

Dr Maxie Maultsby strongly stresses this underlying axiom: *when all the prerequisites for an event are present, that event should, and must, occur.* If this were not so, everything would happen at random. Under those conditions, the human species would quickly perish. You couldn't count on your heart to beat, or your car brakes to work, or your neighbour not to murder you. This insight is axiomatic to any rational view of the world; so let me say it again: if an event occurs, all its prerequisites were present, and the event *should have* occurred. Pursue this idea doggedly until you understand it. Memorize it. Embrace it tightly. And repeat it every day of your life.

So much for glittering generalities. Let's look at how this principle is used in rational self-counselling. Take the case of Angry Arnie (another one of my fictional characters, who is a composite of people I've counselled). Arnie always seems to be mad about something. You won't believe what happened the other day. Arnie bought a shockproof watch. Don't ask me how, but somehow Arnie managed to drop his watch out of a five-storey window. The watch landed on a concrete pavement and shattered in every direction.

Now comes the good part. Can you believe Arnie was furious because his 'shockproof' watch broke? I tried to reason with him. I said to him, 'Look Arnie, given the height of the fall, **Now comes the good part.** the resistance of the pavement, the velocity of the falling watch, the relative masses of watch and pavement, and so forth, your watch *should* have broken.' As usual, Arnie stomped off in a huff.

Is this anecdote a mere caricature? Do you think it's far-fetched? Think about it. Haven't you known people like Arnie? There are countless 'should-ers' in the world who would argue, just as Arnie did, that a watch labelled 'shockproof' shouldn't have broken.

Okay, if you won't buy this example, let me try another. Arnie's sister, Cranky Clara, was working in the kitchen. She dropped an egg, which splattered on the floor. Clara got so mad she grabbed two more eggs and threw them against the wall.

You can tell she's Arnie's sister. I guess she thinks the dropped egg shouldn't have broken. Too bad. If she had been thinking rationally, she would have accepted the fact that a dropped egg should break. If she had been able to think rationally about the mess on her kitchen floor, she would not have made herself angry. As it was, she ended up with three messes instead of one.

Does this example strike close to home? Have you ever got mad enough to break something? How many people have broken knuckles punching doors or walls? Think about it. Have you ever got angry with a friend because they 'should not' have done something? Oh yes, we not only should on broken eggs — we should on people as well.

Should-ing on others is the same mistake we make as when we should on the world. It's equally irrational, unscientific and superstitious. Consider what happened when Arnie, who lives with his sister, came home and saw a slimy mess on the kitchen wall. He blew his top. He shouted, pounded his fists, and cursed Clara, who ran crying to her bedroom.

Arnie frequently gets angry at Clara. He complains that his sister is hopelessly neurotic. But the odd thing is that Arnie complains even more bitterly when Clara behaves neurotically. First, he says she is incurably neurotic. Then he says she shouldn't behave neurotically! Arnie is hard to figure. It seems to me Clara *should* get irrationally angry and throw eggs if she's a hot-tempered screwball who easily gets angry. The way I see it, hot-tempered people should get angry.

Arnie and I often argue about Clara. He claims his sister also is a pathological liar. 'Surely, you will concede,' he argues, 'that Clara shouldn't tell lies to her family and friends.' Arnie always says this with a lofty tone in his voice. You see, Arnie is very self-righteous and moralistic.

Arnie, like many others, believes people should do certain things for reasons of morality. In other words, morality somehow *should* determine what people *should* do — a kind of laying of shoulds on shoulds.

This is unadulterated hokum. Morality cannot bring things into existence except as one part of a vast web of causal prerequisites. Morality can only give people guidelines for action based on a social contract. But whatever people choose to do, their actions will be exactly what they should be. Arnie would be better off focusing on what is, not on what isn't.

This confusion of focus is common among should-ers. They simply are not focused on the problem at hand. Arnie, for example, often directs his attention toward punishing Clara for failing to do what she 'should' do. Arnie screams at his sister and blames her for every household problem. He puts the responsibility entirely on Clara for fulfilling Arnie's wishes. If Arnie were using a rational should, he would accept more responsibility for creating the prerequisites necessary for a smooth-running household. Only then would it be rational to expect things to go smoothly.

> This confusion of focus is common among should-ers.

Suppose Arnie were to tell himself something like this: *Clara has a self-hate problem. That's why she lies so much. She's trying to build up her imaginary self-worth. If I yell at her and tell her she's an ass for lying, she may use my words as material to berate herself even more. Worse yet, she may begin to lie even more than she does now. Considering her distorted thinking, her confusion, her inability to think rationally, it figures she would use lies to protect her mythical self-worth. What I need to do is help her stop being so hard on herself. If she learns to accept her fallibility, perhaps she won't lie so much.*

See how the scientific *should* works to help you take more responsibility for getting what you want? Once Arnie accepts that all the prerequisites for Clara's lying must be present or she wouldn't lie, then he can focus on the causes. Instead of being a little Hitler trying to command something into existence, he can calmly embark on changing what is in his power to change. He plugs himself into a problem-solving mode, an approach that moves him toward his goals while simultaneously reducing his conflicts with his sister.

Reducing conflicts with others, focusing clearly on the problem, assuming responsibility, and eliminating anger are no small benefits. So look carefully for the *shoulds, oughts* and *musts* in your self-talk. If you uncover any magical shoulds, eliminate them. Make an honest person of yourself, and admit you're talking about preferences and desires — not what must be or should exist. Be vigilant. It is all too easy to escalate mere preferences into shoulds. As Dr Karen Horney pointed out in a famous groundbreaking essay, these demands can easily escalate into *the tyranny of the shoulds.*

Remember Sally and her problems with Henry? Sally intuitively knows that our shoulds can tyrannize us. She wishes Henry were more punctual, but she keeps a tight rein on this wish so that it doesn't turn into shoulding. Yes, she often is annoyed. After all, Henry's tardiness can be a hassle — especially when going to movies or concerts. But Sally's irritation, unlike anger, won't prevent her from remaining calm and focusing on the problem.

You can do the same if you monitor your preferences and keep them from growing into demands. Consider the maxim that Dr Albert Ellis commends to all psychotherapists: *Cherchez le should*! Whenever you are upset, look for a should in your thinking or self-talk. You will almost always find one.

Rational shoulds are easy to spot, and they won't cause you any trouble. On the contrary, they'll help you become more lucid, calm, and problem-oriented. They usually have a conditional form: if you do X, then Y will occur. Suppose, for some reason, I wanted to produce steam. If I heat a gallon of water to its boiling point, it should change into steam. If X, then Y. This is a cause-and-effect relationship. Often the if-clause (the condition) is understood. If I say, 'You should boil the water' I am merely omitting the phrase, '...if you want to produce steam.'

We could easily call the scientific should the conditional should, and the magical should the dictatorial should. The conditional should is vastly more useful. After all, looking for connections is part of most problem solving; so don't be self-conscious about using the word 'should'. Worry about the grandiosity reflected in command-oriented self-talk. It's not the words; it's the meaning behind words that gets you in trouble. And, of course, you're the one who gives meaning to your words. Always ask yourself *Am I wishing or am I demanding?*

Jehovian or dictatorial should-ing is intimately connected to intense negative emotions, but the link is strongest in the case of anger. With that in mind, let's trace the various stages of self-talk leading to this destructive emotion. Making yourself angry starts with something very human: you simply want something. We all hope, dream, and desire. Dreaming can be rather pleasant. Much of our daydreaming is filled with wish fulfilment: dreams of being rich, of travelling the world, of having a fabulous lover. There is nothing inherently hurtful in this. But it is a sad fact that healthy wants and dreams are the first step many people take toward ugly feelings of anger.

Our dreams and reality seldom coincide. No matter how hard we work at something, reality usually blocks us from getting everything we want. You may want your spouse or lover to act in certain ways, but he or she will often fail to do so. When wishes are blocked this way, people often say 'I feel frustrated.'

> Our dreams and reality seldom coincide.

Have you ever thought about what 'frustrated' means? Frustration is an important concept; so let's take a moment to precisely define it. You may be in the habit of saying you *feel* frustrated. This, however, will confuse and mislead you. *Frustration is not a feeling.* It is something that stands in your path, something that stops you from getting what you want. In short, it's a part of objective reality that stops you from having your own way. How you feel about a frustration is subjective; the frustration itself is an objective impediment to your wishes.

Suppose your lover doesn't call you as often as you prefer. That's a frustration, not a feeling. You will, however, have some feelings triggered by his or her not calling you — feelings generated by what you say to yourself.

When you face a frustration, you are at a critical point. For if you see your frustration for what it really is — an inconvenience, you will simply feel sad, annoyed, or concerned. But if you tell yourself it's horrible that your lover hasn't called you for a week, you've made your first mistake: you have now made a fine mountain out of a little molehill. You have now started a journey down the road to making yourself angry.

Once you define your frustration as horrible, you will begin to feel bad. Once you start feeling bad, you'll easily slip into the next phase of getting angry. You will tell yourself you shouldn't have to put up with such horrible behaviour. This is a form of shoulding on the world. You may ask yourself 'Why should I have to put up with this rubbish?' Next, you'll start shoulding on your lover. You'll tell yourself things such as, 'He shouldn't act so selfishly and inconsiderately. I deserve better.'

At this point, we can paint a little moustache on you, teach you to goose-step, and pin a swastika on your chest. You now are a little dictator. You not only are desiring, you are demanding. You've changed your wishes into commands, and because you've done so, your previously calm feelings are beginning to simmer. You are on your way to getting truly steamed up.

This will easily get you boiling. But your next piece of foolish thinking will make you blow your stack. So far, you've specifically defined your lover's *behaviour* as terrible. Alas, you won't stop there. Like most people, you overgeneralize and globally rate your lover as terrible. He magically becomes his bad habit; therefore, *he* is now bad.

This idea is a nasty one. Now you're defining somebody you love as bad. Unfortunately, this kind of thought is reduced to a Tarzan-to-Jane type of message as far as Dummibrain is concerned. The emotion-brain hears something like *John bad. John bad for me. John my enemy*. Dummibrain feels threatened when facing an enemy and starts pushing your fight-or-flight buttons. Your adrenaline starts churning. You begin to feel your anger physically. You get a headache, heartburn, insomnia — even that old knee injury starts hurting again.

With the steam shooting out of your ears, you're ready for the last link in your chain of nutty thoughts: 'He's a rotten s.o.b. for making me suffer like this, and he's going to pay for it. If it's the last thing I do, I'll get even with that louse.' This kind of self-talk promotes all sorts of delicious fantasies, from hanging him by the thumbs to giving him the cold shoulder when he's in the mood for love.

This escalation of your feelings is often one part of a triad of escalation. One, you escalate your thoughts.

This escalation of your feelings is often one part of a triad of escalation.

Two, as your thoughts escalate, your anger escalates. Three, you escalate your behaviour.

Feeling resentful, you now behave coldly toward your lover, maybe even nastily. Perhaps you tell him he's self-centered and selfish. As you might expect, that puts the fat in the fire. Feeling wounded by your words, your lover withdraws and calls you even less than before. Congratulations — now you have three problems where once you had only one: first, your lover isn't calling you as often as you prefer, second, he is apparently miffed at you, and third, you feel rotten.

It is this escalation of behaviour that makes anger a dangerous and destructive emotion. Our prisons are full of angry criminals — men who early in life acquired a Jehovah complex. Anger is the primary cause of child abuse, wife beating, divorce, murder and assault. Countless other social maladies have hidden connections to anger. Robbery, rape, and vandalism have a core of anger. On hot days, automobile accidents increase significantly as tempers rise. Suicide is often motivated by anger toward a spouse or parents. Countless fires are set by vengeful crackpots. Cruelty to dumb animals is a frequent outlet for anger. Our courts are swamped with angry lawsuits. The list is endless.

Anger is clearly the most destructive emotion. Its disadvantages for your personal growth and well-being are many in number. To give you a better idea of these disadvantages, I've prepared a list. I call it 'anger's dirty dozen'. Several of these items are restatements of points made by Dr Albert Ellis. Others are results of my own observations.

These are a few of anger's ignoble spin-offs. They don't, however, include any of the drawbacks you inflict on those around you. Your children may imitate you and grow up to be angry adults. Your spouse may develop ulcers. Even your cat may become neurotic and pee in your shoes. The truth is most of us adjust poorly to the irascibility of a chronically angry person.

So much for the drawbacks. Does anger have any advantages? Maybe. A soldier in hand-to-hand combat might find anger useful. Sometimes we can use anger to bully another person into compliance with our wishes. Blowing off steam can feel good, at

Anger's Dirty Dozen

1. When angry, you misfocus. You equate a person with his actions. You then feel hostile toward the total person, not just his behaviour.

2. Since this person will want to protect his imaginary self-worth, he may respond defensively, rather than helpfully.

3. Anger can affect your behaviour toward innocent people. You may yell at the kids, snap at your spouse, and argue with your neighbour.

4. They, in turn, will act hostile toward you.

5. As more people dislike and shun you, you'll probably dump on yourself, an action that will only add to your emotional turmoil.

6. Depression and anxiety usually follow close on the heels of anger. As a result, you may foul up other areas of your life.

7. Anger has a way of lingering long after the original problem has cleared up.

8. When you're angry, you become blind to the weaknesses of your own position. This tunnel vision handicaps your learning and growth.

9. Once you're angry, you tend to focus on real or imagined revenge, rather than focusing on your problem.

10. When angry, you tend to deny you're emotionally disturbed. This keeps you from processing your nutty thinking.

11. Anger can cause serious physical illness.

12. If you have a habit of breaking things when angry, it can be tough on the budget.

least momentarily. Sometimes we feel ashamed after a violent tantrum and do some constructive introspection. Such a post-mortem may give us a few insights into our demandingness. As you can see, I'm stretching. The bottom line is that anger has few, if any, clear-cut advantages.

We can safely say that 95% of the time, at least in civilized society, anger gives little benefit and does much harm. You can almost invariably find healthier alternatives to making yourself angry. By avoiding anger, you will almost certainly do better at solving your problems and getting what you want. Rage, vengeance, aggression — these are all self-defeating in the long run.

Take aggression. Many believe we need to be aggressive to get what we want in the world. Those who think aggression is therapeutic seem to lump aggression and assertion together. But assertiveness is manifestly different from aggressiveness. Assertiveness, as taught by rational therapists, is used to get what you want and to stop others from acting unfairly toward you.

Admittedly, in these respects, assertiveness sounds much like aggressiveness. It differs, however, in that it respects the rights of others. It doesn't include the bullying of others or putting them down. It sees people as distinct from their acts. If somebody acts badly toward me, I can be assertive without being negative toward a total person. Assertiveness recognizes that all human beings are fallible and are not equal to a few mistakes or a single bad behaviour.

Assertiveness is positive, while aggression is negative. Aggression equates a person with his or her bad act and puts down the entire person as well as the offending behaviour.

> Assertiveness is positive, while aggression is negative.

Aggression shoulds on people. It holds that others must not act badly toward me or frustrate my aims. Aggression, therefore, is irrational. Rational assertiveness, in contrast, holds that human mistakes happen because they must happen. This doesn't mean it lets people off the hook; it simply doesn't demonize people. Instead of focusing on people, assertiveness focuses on unwanted behaviour.

Aggression is often passive and indirect. It disguises itself, and doesn't openly declare what is wanted. A passive aggressor is sometimes so dishonest, they won't even admit to themself what they want. Rational assertiveness is honest. An assertive person is frank in saying what they want, what they dislike, and what they feel.

Aggressors are often self-righteous. They allow little room for the possibility they have failed to understand somebody. They are angry, and their anger rests on Jehovian grandiosity. Self-assertiveness is calm and open-minded. That is not to say it is namby-pamby. Acceptance of human fallibility doesn't make you a wimp.

Aggressors are accusatory, often loudly so. Self-assertors speak calmly in a normal tone of voice. Sometimes they are empathic and supportive of the other person, if not of his or her actions.

Aggressors demand that others always treat them with absolute justice and fairness. When treated unfairly, they whiningly tell themselves they can't stand it. A rationally assertive person wants to be treated fairly, but they accept the fact that others often do act unfairly. They know they can stand it. They are determined to challenge unfairness, but they know they can live with it if they have to.

In summary, if you apply rational self-talk to the goal of getting what you want, you can become an assertive person. When you use irrational self-talk, you may easily become an aggressive person. Aggressive people often get what they want, but usually at a high cost. Reaching for your goals with rational assertiveness can also get you what you want, but with less pain and disruption.

I've taken the time to amply describe rational self-assertiveness because its absence can be a major contributor to anger. If you fail to assert your rights, you will tend to feel 'used'. This leads to horribilizing, should-ing and condemning. The result is anger toward the person who is 'using' you.

Please note that I am careful to place quotation marks around 'using'. This is because the idea that somebody is 'using' you is almost always irrational. We are almost never used by other people.

Here's a colourful example I've used with support groups. Imagine you're in an empty room with Big John, a defensive tackle for the Los Angeles Roughnecks. Imagine that a flash fire occurs. The doorway is blocked by flames. Big John decides to jump out of the window, but the closed window is stuck. John figures he'll cut himself if he jumps through the glass. If nothing else, Big John is practical. He bodily picks you up and hurls you through the window. He then leaps through the window unscathed by fire or broken glass. No question about it: John has used you.

Now suppose Big John is in the room with a beautiful, seductive model. She doesn't want to jump first for fear of cutting her face. She tells John he should go first because it doesn't matter if a football player has a scarred face. She promises John undying love and many titillating nights if he goes first; so the smitten John does what she asks of him. Not unexpectedly, he cuts his face.

Following this, the model decides she actually has no desire to see John again. John, of course, is not very happy about this turn of events. He broods long and hard. He tells himself, 'Jumping through that glass and cutting myself was a nasty experience. I hate the scars I have. It's that scumbag's fault. She used me. What a rotten bitch. She deserves to burn in hell. I'm gonna get even with her one way or another.'

Do you see the difference? In the first case, you had no choice. You were unwillingly thrown through a window. In the second case, John voluntarily jumped through the window. Admittedly, these choices are not very attractive; nonetheless, they are real choices.

Sometimes we struggle over choices that are invitingly attractive, such as choosing between two succulent desserts on the menu. Some choices don't even seem like choices. If, for example, you win the state lottery, you face the decision of whether to claim the prize money or not. Most of the choices we wrestle with, however, are not so happy.

Think about the kind of options you typically face. Should I mow the lawn or paint the garage? Wash the car or weed the garden? Work on Saturday or lose the overtime pay? Go through the hassle of seeing a doctor or wait out a nasty case of flu? Get a divorce or struggle on with a failing marriage? Get high risk lower-back surgery or put up with a bad back? Stay with a boring-but-secure job or take an exciting-but-insecure job? And so forth.

If you're old enough to remember the Jack Benny radio show, you may remember a famous skit where Jack, a legendary skin-flint, is approached by a robber. The thief says to him, 'Your money or your life!' There is a long pause. The impatient thief growls, 'Well?' Jack screams, 'I'm thinking, I'm thinking!' The humour comes partly from the fact we don't think of this as a choice. You see, if one alternative is exceptionally bad, we see ourselves as forced to pick the lesser of two evils. Nonetheless, it is a choice.

Think about it. How about the soldier who throws himself on a hand grenade to save his buddies? History has many examples of heroic sacrifices of life. These were choices. If not, wherein lies the heroism? So even in the most extreme case, where death is one of the options, it is still a choice.

My point is that you should resist the temptation to see yourself as being 'used' by others. If you make the choice to do something, admit to yourself that you chose to do so. If you chose to do so through a fear of disapproval, then tackle this as a separate neurotic problem. Instead of brooding over having been 'used' and thereby diminished, rethink your nutty belief in self-worth. Above all, learn to be rationally self-assertive.

> My point is that you should resist the temptation to see yourself as being 'used' by others.

There it is again. Self-worth. Have you noticed how this goblin keeps popping up? It seems to be an omnipresent ghost haunting every nook and cranny of our psyche. We get depressed when we think we don't have it. We get scared when we think we might lose it. We get angry when... Well, this link is a little harder to explain. As you will see, the connection with anger is far more subtle.

Let's revisit Angry Arnie. When Arnie gets mad at his sister, we can count on finding four items in his self-talk:

1. *This is horrible!*
2. *I can't deal with this.*
3. *She shouldn't do this.*
4. *She's a real bitch and deserves to be punished.*

Normally, one could overcome one's anger by replacing this script with rational thoughts. But if that fails, and the anger remains, it's a good idea to start digging for self-worth issues. In the case of Arnie, we would find that Arnie is doing some additional magicking: he is laying his ego on the line. When Clara behaves contrary to his wishes he sees himself as being diminished. Arnie unwittingly and mystically makes his self-worth depend on Clara's actions.

Is it any wonder Arnie obsessively monitors Clara's behaviour? If she does something contrary to his wishes, he sees his self-worth as eroded. Arnie carries a performance evaluation form in his head. If Clara's actions enlarge his self-worth, she gets an A. If her actions diminish his self-worth, she gets an F, not to mention the flak she gets from Arnie.

Here's how this might work. Arnie and Clara have a well-established custom of going out for Sunday brunch. One day Clara acquires a lover and starts having Sunday brunch with him instead of Arnie. Arnie sees himself as put down. His self-worth is mystically endangered, and he starts throwing temper tantrums — much to the amazement of Clara. After all, she's been looking for a boyfriend for a long time. She's very happy with her new love affair, and she's deeply disappointed by her brother's reaction.

This habit of attaching one's ego to another's behaviour and then getting angry when that person's behaviour doesn't comply with one's wishes is what I call *ego anger*. This anger uses the same basic script as most anger, but it adds thoughts such as, *She's putting me down. He's making a fool of me.* Put in modern psychobabble, the thoughts may sound like this: *I'm being discounted. I'm being invalidated. I'm being disempowered.* And so forth.

Ego anger seems to have more intensity than simple Jehovian anger. The deep bitterness marking many divorces often has links with self-worth issues. When men kill or maim one another in barroom fights, their rage often stems from self-worth obsessions. Hell hath no fury like a person robbed of his or her self-worth. So if you're having trouble overcoming your anger with ordinary anti-anger scripts, reread Chapter 2 and work on writing some scripts debunking the myth of self-worth.

Ego anger can erode the relationship you have with your lover, your boss, your co-workers, or your kids. Watch out for ego anger at the workplace. It's especially common to equate

Ego anger can erode the relationship you have with your lover, your boss, your co-workers, or your kids.

one's mythical self-worth with one's job performance. This can make you angrily resistant to criticism — an attitude that can sabotage your career.

Parenting can also be sabotaged by ego anger. Some parents feel irrationally put down when their children are disobedient or mischievous. The Jehovah complex shows up easily when you're trying to keep your kids in line. If you get intensely angry at your children, start searching for a Jehovian should. Then work on a new parenting script purged of should-ing. If you continue to have an anger problem, keep looking for hidden self-worth issues. These potent catalysts often hide in the dark corners of our self-talk.

Our most damaging self-talk is a shadowy presence. Some meanings are coyly unverbalized. When I refer to these furtive, unspoken beliefs, I use the word *attitudes* and reserve the word *beliefs* for more overt thoughts. This distinction, however, is mostly one of convenience and is imprecise at best. My point is that we have to use more sophisticated detective work to locate and articulate attitudes. After all, we don't normally talk to ourselves with sentences such as, *Egad! She's robbing me of my self-worth.*

Fortunately, not all your detective work will be this challenging. Take the subterfuge of rhetorical questions. These little gimmicks often show up in our self-talk. I label them rhetorical because they are ersatz questions — hypocritical queries asked only as ways to express feelings or as disguises for bizarre thoughts.

Consider *what-if* questions. They look like this: *What if my husband is having an affair? What if I fail this exam? What if I ask Kathy out and she turns me down? What if I make a fool of myself when we go roller-skating? What if...* Odd as it may seem, we seldom answer these questions.

So what should we do with these fake questions when we find them in our self-talk? Some therapists recommend answering them whenever they appear. I think this is generally useful, but I have some reservations about always responding to these *what-if* questions.

People who are compulsive *what-iffers* have a possibilistic outlook on life. They embrace any wild possibility floating by in the stream of consciousness. This means many of their rhetorical questions are stunningly wacko. If you merely give a rational answer to a daffy question, you may over-dignify it. More than being a question, it may be an underlying crazy thought that needs to be exposed and processed.

So how do you expose such a thought? Easily. Simply convert the question into a statement. Permit me to illustrate with a case study. A middle-aged woman in one of my support groups presented this problem. Her daughter lived in a distant city, and the mother had anxiety attacks every time her daughter flew to visit her. With a little probing, the anxiety-provoking thought was found in the form of a what-if question. While awaiting her daughter's arrival, she would say to herself, 'What if my daughter's plane has crashed?'

I asked her if she had ever answered the question. She said no. In fact, it had never occurred to her to do so. At this point, I had to choose between the two methods of tackling a what-if question: either answer it rationally or translate it into a statement. I decided against dignifying her pseudo-question with an answer and opted for the translation method. I suggested to the woman that she convert the question into a statement whenever it popped up in her self-talk.

Rendered as a flat declaration, her question becomes, 'My daughter's plane has crashed.' This brings the irrationality of the thought into strong relief. I wanted the woman to see that her underlying belief was baseless. After all, she did not have a shred of evidence to suggest her daughter's plane had crashed.

I further suggested she take a paper and pencil and write down a two-column, for-and-against tally of evidence. She was to make a list of all the reasons for believing the plane had crashed. Next to that column, she was to make a list of all the reasons for believing the plane had not plummeted to earth. She went home and used this method the next time her daughter flew to see her. She later reported to the support group that she had been unable to think of a single rational reason to support the belief that her daughter's plane had crashed. On the other hand, she had easily come up with a host of reasons for assuming her daughter was alive and unharmed. As you might guess, she started feeling much calmer.

What this woman did was to simply use the empirical method. She noted how much counted for her belief and how much counted against it. She created a long list of reasons counting against her anxiety-triggering belief. In contrast, she did not find a scintilla of evidence supporting her fanciful thought. Once the groundless thought was refuted, she became calm. You see, for all practical purposes, her anxious thought *was* her anxiety. Once the thought was gone, the anxiety was gone.

> **What this woman did was to simply use the empirical method.**

This is one of the great insights discovered by Dr Albert Ellis in the 1950s. I urge you to ponder this groundbreaking discovery. It will give you an elementary understanding of what emotions are. I am convinced your new insight will put you ahead of many professionals. I once was listening to an advice radio show run by a famous psychologist. A caller asked her, 'Doctor, could you please tell me what emotions are?' This famous radio shrink stammered and stalled and waffled. Finally, she admitted she didn't know what emotions were! Yet she was on the air telling people how to manage their emotions.

The insights provided by Dr Ellis are what enabled me to help the woman who was anxious over her daughter's plane trips. I knew that as she dissolved the irrational thought generating her anxiety, she would simultaneously dissolve her anxiety. To help her unseat her irrational emotion-thought, I merely showed her a simple use of the scientific method.

This use of the scientific method is what rational self-counselling is all about. Use the empirical method, and use it

vigorously. Ask yourself repeatedly *Where's my proof? What
evidence do I have that this is
true? Why should I believe this?
Is this probable? Or highly
improbable? What are the chances of this being true? One in a
million? One in ten million? Or one in a trillion?*

> This use of the scientific method is what rational self-counselling is all about.

The number of bad things that can happen in your life is
astronomical. To stew over possible happenings is to be perpetu-
ally anxious. You will never run out of things to worry about. Do
you think your worrying will prevent bad things from happening? Don't pooh-pooh this question, and don't think I'm being
patronizing. If you're a chronic worrier, the truth is you probably
do believe worrying will prevent nasty events.

Although they are unaware of having this superstition, many
worriers use their anxiety as a form of voodoo for controlling
objective reality. They unwittingly believe they can control the
laws of cause and effect with their endless nail-biting.

How is this nutty superstition born? Ironically, it seems to
come from a goofy use of empirical evidence. What if every time
you left your house, you worried that your house might be burning down while you were away? Suppose you did this 1,000
times. Now suppose you returned home 1,000 times to find your
house still standing. Somewhere, at some level of thought, you
will have perceived this sequence of events: (1) I worry about my
house being on fire, and (2) every time I worry, no fire occurs.

When this sequence repeats itself over and over, you may be
conditioned to feel there is a cause-and-effect relationship. Soon
you become afraid of not being afraid. After all, why give up a
good system? If it works, why question it? If it ain't broke, don't
fix it. This mindless conditioning leads one to accept a totally
needless anxiety.

If you're a worrier who wants to live less fearfully, start expos-
ing and attacking the unspoken notion that you can control
reality through nail-biting or any other hocus-pocus.

If you like a more structured approach to replacing screwy
scripts, you may find the following paradigm useful. Study the
model sentences carefully. Then memorize them.

Self-talk	
Magical	**Rational**
This is horrible.	I dislike this.
I can't stand this.	I'll live through this.
This shouldn't happen.	This should happen.
He is a bad person.	He did something bad.

Now expand on each magical belief. State as simply as you can why the belief is irrational. Then expand on each rational belief. State as simply as you can why the belief is rational.

Now apply the paradigm to real people or events. *Important*: don't use events or situations that are exceptionally stressful. It's better to use minor problems when you are first practising your self-counselling.

Here's how Angry Arnie filled in the chart after Clara forgot his birthday.

Self-talk	
Magical	**Rational**
1. How horrible of Clara to forget my birthday.	1. I'm disappointed Clara forgot my birthday.
2. I can't stand her selfishness.	2. Her forgetfulness won't kill me.
3. She certainly should remember my birthday.	3. Clara is very forgetful. It figures she would forget my birthday.
4. What a bitch she is.	4. Clara is a fallible human being; therefore, she forgets things.

You can vary this exercise by doing it with three columns, the middle column being a list of challenges to your magical thoughts. The first item might look something like this on a three-column chart:

Magical thought	Challenge thought	Rational
1. This is horrible.	1. Horribleness doesn't exist.	1. I'm disappointed.

Don't hesitate to flesh out this skeletal model. Try to do one chart daily. You'll find countless little problems to practise on. Don't worry about how small the problem is. Using minor hassles for practice has a prophylactic effect. You will be better prepared for life's major problems if you practise first with little problems.

At first, you might try putting a sample chart on a recipe card and carrying it with you. Whenever a small problem arises, you can pull out your card and mentally create a self-talk script appropriate to the problem at hand.

For starters you have only four things to chip away at: (1) exaggerating (2) telling yourself you can't cope (3) should-ing and (4) globally condemning people.

Put another way, you have four *don'ts* to observe: don't horribilize, don't say you can't cope, don't should, and don't put down anybody, including yourself.

You might find it beneficial to periodically re-read my discussions on the myth of self-worth and the two kinds of shoulds. These two concepts cause the most difficulty. The best way to master these slippery ideas is to read and re-read, think and re-think, discuss and re-discuss. In other words, hammer yourself with repetition, repetition, repetition.

While most of the tools we use in rational self-counselling are simple, the job of tearing down and rebuilding your irrational self-talk is hard work. The method is simple, that is to say simple to understand. But it is hard in the sense it requires hard work. The choice is yours. You can choose emotional pain or choose a path of hard work that leads to emotional peace.

Oddly enough, many people make the choice to keep their old ways. This is notably so where the Jehovah complex is concerned. Why? Mainly because Jehovian anger has certain payoffs. Take the case of people saddled with long-term frustrations. They sometimes start seeing themselves as helpless and powerless. As you might expect, this triggers anxiety.

This state of anxiety, in turn, often leads to anger. This happens because anger is an excellent masking emotion. In our culture, anger is seen as a strong emotion, while fear is seen as a weak emotion. It's no surprise that many anxious people are quick to anger themselves. What better way to cover up feelings that are held in contempt by our society.

In addition to cloaking anxiety, anger makes us feel as though we're doing something. It seems better than just sitting on one's rear and feeling helpless. If we throw things around or break a few dishes, we feel more powerful. Momentarily, we feel as though we've gained greater control over our environment. This is reinforced when we note that violent anger often intimidates those around us. These factors combine to give us a fleeting illusion of greater strength — a deception that alleviates feelings of unworthiness. Have you been noticing how often issues of self-worth arise?

> In addition to cloaking anxiety, anger makes us feel as though we're doing something.

This form of anger is often at the core of what is called 'righteous anger'. It inflates our sense of self-worth by helping us to believe we are the bearers of righteousness — defenders of God, mother, and country. With this heady attitude, we can inflate our self-worth to a bursting point.

Righteous anger is especially visible among militant reformers. These people think anger is necessary to galvanize their followers and effect social reform. At first glance, there seems to be a seed of truth in this. This, however, is true only if you believe passive indifference is the sole alternative. The truth is if you strongly want social change, anger is not the only or best tool. I maintain that angry reformers are selling a false dilemma that posits either angry aggression or wimpy surrender to injustice. As you will see, we can easily go between the horns of this dilemma.

Angry people are not the best reformers. They tend to stew excessively in their own anger. They often spend more time ranting about injustice than trying to correct it. In other words, they are not sufficiently problem-focused. Sure, they rave plenty about injustice, but they do little else.

Effective social reformers usually are calm, determined people. They expend most of their energy on the tactical and strategic problems of reform. Martin Luther King, who was a masterful tactician, was not an angry man. Yet he changed the USA forever. Lenin was not an angry man, but he changed the history of the world. Mahatma Gandhi was not an angry man, but he brought the mighty British Empire to its knees.

Don't buy the myth you need anger to act effectively. You will be far more effective if you are calm and determined. Those reformers who exude righteous anger are especially blind to the weaknesses of their positions. As a result, they never seem to foresee the effects of their actions. The French revolutionaries did not foresee the bloody consequences of their revolution. Hitler and Mussolini were angry reformers who never foresaw the cataclysmic results of their revolutions. Social changes born in a caldron of rage seldom lead to beneficial change.

This lack of foresight occurs in our personal lives. If you make drastic changes in the heat of anger, you may not act in your own best interest. Calm determination will do more to effect valuable and lasting changes in your life.

Whether you have this kind of resoluteness depends on how you organize, measure, and relate to reality. The Jehovah complex fosters a mystical view of reality. Under the aegis of its disturbed grandiosity, we believe that reality should accommodate itself to what we want. If we want X, then X somehow must be or should be. This is the fundamental *non sequitur* of the Jehovah complex.

If we want the world to be fair — doesn't everybody? — it does not follow that the world *should* be fair. It does not follow that human beings should act honorably because we demand that they do so. It does not follow that the laws of the universe should be suspended in answer to our whining.

You can pound your breast, tear your hair, and scream like a tortured banshee. It matters not. The laws of physics will go on, indifferent to your bootless cries. Your anger will change nothing about the way reality operates. You will, however, profoundly vitiate your own happiness.

As I end this chapter, I leave you with one of my favorite epigrams.

Anger is a means to punish ourselves for the actions of others.

5

I Can't Live Without You

6 The mind itself wants nothing, unless it creates a want for itself. 9

Marcus Aurelius

Most people in our society mindlessly pay homage to the belief that we need other people. In fact, this belief has become sacrosanct among many in the counselling professions. When I publicly reject this sacred cow, my remarks trigger an amazing amount of anger; nonetheless, the widely held article of faith that 'people need people' is clearly false. Indeed, I hope to show you that people who need people are far from being 'the luckiest people in the world'.

Think for a moment about the meaning of *need*. I'm sure you'll agree a need is something you *must* have. To say you must have something is to say you cannot survive without it. You cannot, for example, live without water. You cannot live without food. You cannot live without oxygen. And, in many places, you cannot long endure without shelter.

Now suppose I were to add to this list, 'You cannot live without a love companion.' The five *musts* for human survival would read: food, water, oxygen, shelter and a lover. Does this sound a wee bit odd? I hope so. Yet countless people unwittingly cling to this belief with the fervour of a drowning person clutching a lifebelt.

Why do people adhere so fanatically to a belief that is obviously false? A key factor is the ubiquitous presence of the myth of self-worth. As we know, one of the main avenues to self-worth is to be loved and 'needed' by other people. I regret to say that many people in the mental health profession share this irrational belief. I've seen some of them stalk out of lectures by Dr Albert Ellis, furious at the founding father of rational psychotherapy for daring to question the hallowed canon: *people need people*. (I suspect some of these professionals secretly harbour the corollary: *My clients need me.*)

If you're feeling outraged and feel like walking out on me, please be patient while I approach the issue from another direction. For the time being, I'll postpone discussing the truth or falsity of the people-need-people belief. Instead, we'll look at this creed pragmatically. What are the consequences of holding such a belief? How do the advantages stack up against the disadvantages? Is it a useful belief? Once we answer these questions, we can return to considering whether the belief is true or not. For starters, let's simply take a look at a half-dozen ways that holding this belief can impinge on a person's life.

Let's begin by considering the case of Anxious Annie. Annie strongly believes she needs other people. In other words, she believes she *must* have the affection, support and approval of other people. And I don't mean just some people — Annie craves the approval of all of the people all of the time. In fact, Annie not only craves this approval, she demands it. After all, this is a matter of survival for Annie's worthiness.

So Annie works hard at getting approval from others. At first glance, she simply seems like a warm, pliable and giving person. But as one watches her more closely, one is tempted to use adjectives such as *servile* or *fawning*. She seems unable to say no to anybody and is involved in a legion of volunteer activities. In fact, she is so busy with these duties she has practically no time to spend with her family or to pursue any of her own interests.

If you watch Annie socializing at a party, you will notice she seems to agree with anything anybody says. If somebody says we should sign a test-ban treaty to halt all nuclear testing, Annie fervently agrees. If she moves to the other side of the room, and somebody is saying we should continue developing and testing our nuclear weapons, Annie nods her head energetically. Anybody watching Annie would think she had no mind of her own.

Actually, Annie is bright and articulate. She simply is afraid of disapproval. Believing she must have the approval of others at all times, Annie has turned herself into a bore. This is one of the costs of believing one needs other people.

Using a cost-benefit analysis, we quickly see a second disadvantage of the I-need-other-people belief. The opinions, wants, and growth of other people take precedence over one's own growth. Annie has some real talent as a writer, and she derives great joy from writing. But she spends so much time volunteering and doing favours, she has little time to work on things that interest her or stimulate her own growth. She lets her own potential shrivel in a frantic effort to be all things to all people.

Nor is this the only baneful spin-off from her belief that she needs other people. As we observe Annie, we notice a third mischief spawned by her neediness. Annie's husband is an angry man who sometimes belts her when he's been drinking. Annie has put up with this abuse for years. Many of her friends have urged her to leave her husband. But Annie believes she needs him. She fears she cannot survive without him, either emotionally or financially. So she tolerates unfairness, verbal cruelty, and even physical abuse. This kind of mistreatment is a burden often borne by those who believe they need other people.

Consider still another drawback in our ugly list: Annie is extremely moody. Her obsessive need for strokes keeps her on an emotional roller coaster. Believing she needs the love of others, she constantly monitors their behaviour to see if they're acting in a positive, loving way toward her. When others do what she wants, her mood ranges from mildly happy to elated. When they don't behave the way she wants, she often sinks into a tearful, distraught mood. In short, Annie is an emotional yo-yo.

We might be tempted to ask who is yanking Annie's yo-yo string, but we already know Annie generates her own blues through what she says to Dummibrain. At the moment, we're interested in when it is that Annie becomes morose, not how she upsets herself. We find this to be readily observable. She depresses herself when others push her buttons. Bear in mind that others can do this only indirectly and only because she empowers them to do so.

This brings us to number five in the litany of damages done by the people-need-people belief. By allowing others to pull her strings, Annie makes herself a puppet. She yields control over her own emotional destiny to other people. Annie is a classic example of a dependent person.

We often see this kind of emotional dependency in romantic love. Have you ever had a lover who was extremely moody? This was probably because his or her moods were chained to your behaviour. When

> **We often see this kind of emotional dependency in romantic love.**

you were affectionate or sexual, your lover wore a smile. Whenever you were lost in your thoughts or focusing on a problem, your partner's smile quickly vanished.

Is it possible you are excessively moody when involved in an affair? Take a cold, clinical look at your past romantic behaviours. If you've been excessively moody, start probing your self-talk. Perhaps you've been using scripts suffused with neediness and demandingness. If you suspect this is the case, take the time to write some rational scripts and practise them persistently, especially if you're experiencing a rocky relationship.

Extreme dependency is capsulized in this phrase: *I can't live without you.* Admittedly, this is poetic licence of the kind used by lovers when their glands are bubbling. The thinking brain certainly understands this amative puffery. But not Dummibrain. He'll take this poetry literally and push the panic button every time your lover seems withdrawn — not to mention when he or she is angry.

Take Anxious Annie. Every time her husband is angry, Annie thinks, 'Oh, my God. He's pushing me away. I wonder if he's thinking about leaving me. Suppose he does? What would I do? I couldn't bear being alone and unloved.' And so forth. I'm sure you've heard people talking this way. Maybe you've had similar thoughts yourself. If so, you need to do some serious overhauling of your relationship scripts.

This kind of emotional dependency brings us to our sixth disadvantage — a drawback that is a close corollary of emotional dependency. If you are in an intimate relationship, and you tend to be emotionally dependent, your lover will quickly sense this. Willy-nilly he or she will soon instinctively learn how to control you. How? By using emotional blackmail. Simply put, you do what your partner wants, or your normally warm lover withdraws from you.

Actually, a lover doesn't have to withdraw. Your lover merely has to send subtle signals to the effect that he or she might withdraw. Emotional blackmail is common in love relationships. Mind you, I'm not describing something sinister or malicious. Often the blackmailer is unaware of what he or she is doing. Most people instinctively sense dependency, and they tend to instinctively cash in on the benefits. Think about it, and be honest. Have you ever exploited this trait in others to get what you wanted? Have others ever exploited your neediness?

Susceptibility to emotional blackmail completes our list of disadvantages. Let's not, however, forget the points I covered in Chapter 2. The belief that one needs other people has close ties to the myth of self-worth. I stressed to you that fear of disapproval can cause you to focus on how **well** you are doing, rather than on **what** you are doing. I also said fear of disapproval can turn you into a timid mouse afraid to try new experiences.

Now let's add these two disadvantages and review the list of liabilities spawned by the popular belief that people need people, and, as Barbra Streisand would have us believe, 'People who need people are the luckiest people in the world'.

I promised to postpone arguing the validity of the belief that we need other people while we looked at some of the disadvantages incurred by holding this belief. I think you'll agree that the following list of drawbacks makes the I-need-people creed risky. With that in mind, I hope you're now ready to re-examine the validity of this popular doctrine. After all, if holding a belief has the potential to undermine your emotional health, you had best take a long, hard look at its soundness. Furthermore, we know from considerable clinical experience that if a belief is emotionally harmful, the chances are extremely high that it's a false or highly irrational belief.

Spin-offs from holding the belief 'I need other people'

1. You may become a fawning bore.

2. You may tend to ignore your own self-growth while aiding the growth of others.

3. You may become a doormat for others who mistreat you.

4. You may become moody as you focus obsessively on how others behave toward you.

5. You may become overly dependent.

6. You may easily become a victim of emotional blackmail.

7. You may start focusing on how well you're doing rather than on what you are doing.

8. You may become timid about trying new experiences.

Having cautiously paved the way, I now want to consider the literal truth or falsity of the common belief that we need other people. First, let's bring it down to earth by looking at concrete examples. Take the case of Clingy Cleo. She deeply believes she *needs* her boyfriend. She has often said she would die if he ever left her. Yes, we know Cleo is using 'die' metaphorically. Even so, the metaphor is rather overblown. Perhaps she would deeply miss him if they separated. She would likely miss sex, companionship, and sharing problems with an intimate partner. These are important and valuable, but do they justify using terms such as *die*?

Cleo might argue she means 'die' in a psychological sense. But how exactly does one die psychologically? This is psychobabble. Does she mean she would perish in some mystical or existential sense? Again, what does that mean? Cleo would still be Cleo. Nothing would be subtracted from her. She is five feet five inches tall. If her lover leaves her, she will still be five feet five inches tall. She has blonde hair and blue eyes. If her lover leaves her, she will still have blonde hair and blue eyes. She will still be Cleo and nobody else. She will not be destroyed, diminished, or objectively altered by her lover's rejection.

An attractive and highly intelligent model once told me her ex-lover had 'destroyed' her by dumping her. She was suffering from severe anxiety and was using drugs in a fruitless quest for serenity. I was not surprised that she felt anxious. Try telling Dummibrain somebody has 'destroyed' you, and watch your anxiety soar. I guarantee you that you'll feel fearful if you brainwash yourself with the notion that your lover can destroy you.

How did a bright woman like this buy into such obvious hokum? I immediately looked for feelings of worthlessness. The myth of self-worth is usually lurking somewhere when a person claims to be devastated by a rejection. People who feel insecure often think they can augment their self-worth through other people. My otherwise intelligent client had unthinkingly bought into the myth of self-worth. She was desperately convinced she had to have this elusive, phantasmal something.

This woman, like Clingy Cleo, carries a big sign in her head that looks like this:

> A woman without a man is a zero.
> I am a woman without a man.
> Therefore, I am a zero.

This kind of superstitious syllogism partly explains why so many young people rush into marriage. Many teenagers haven't learned to accept themselves with all their warts and foibles. They desperately search for a way to win their mythical self-worth. A teenager yearning for a sense of self-worth will often look for it in another person, a lover he blindly idealizes. The idealized qualities of this idol are expected to somehow endow the teenager with greater worth. This is why the disillusionment is so great when he discovers his mate is a fallible human being. Not only does his idol have feet of clay, this sad youngster has failed to attain the illusory self-worth he so desperately longed for.

This screwy method for seeking self-worth often is reinforced by a fear of appearing different. Historically, women have been especially prone to this. Early in life a female is often fed a pabulum of rescue fantasies: Cinderella, Sleeping Beauty, Snow White, Rapunzel, and so forth. On the surface, she dreams of rescue from singlehood, while what she truly craves is to be rescued from unworthiness, the shame that comes from remaining single while all her friends are finding their knights in shining armour. For these grieving Cinderellas, singlehood is an ugly disfigurement, while a wedding ring is a badge of worthiness.

Escape from singlehood endows self-worth in two ways: (1) you earn it vicariously through an idealized mate who loves you, or (2) you win it through the approbation of your peers. Alas, the illusion fades quickly. Early marriage often become a painful entanglement of the neurotic problems each youngster brings to the relationship.

The dotty belief that your mate can endow you with greater worthiness has an ugly flip side: your mate can also take it away. This often generates a destructive game married people play. Let's call it the **blame game**. It usually has five steps similar to these:

1. You demand that your partner constantly love and adore you so as to keep your self-worth replenished.
2. When he fails to do so, you get anxious over your shrinking self-worth.
3. You brood and suffer over your loss.
4. You blame your mate for the suffering and conclude he is cruel.
5. You punish your mate with sarcasm or by giving him the cold shoulder when he is in the mood for love.

The blame game is a chief cause of static marriages, partnerships that never grow. The blame game grows out of focusing excessively on your mate's behaviour. You blame your spouse for your every pain and for causing every quarrel. Sometimes both partners do this. This means neither spouse gets in touch with what he or she is doing to block the relationship; consequently, neither works to change his or her mistaken behaviour. Neither partner grows, and the marriage strangles in a web of neurotic conflict.

Remember that a relationship doesn't exist in the abstract. It's a merging of two sets of objective behaviour. For this merger to work, each spouse must focus on what he or she is doing to handicap the marriage, not on how one's spouse is impeding the marriage. To avoid the blame game, consistently ask yourself, *What am I doing to block this relationship?* Then ask yourself, *How can I change what I'm doing?* Admittedly it's best when both partners do this, but a marriage gone astray often can be saved if only one person learns to focus on his or her own behaviour. Keep reminding yourself you can only control your own actions.

If the blame game continues, divorce is likely. This rupture is one of the ugly experiences few people are prepared to cope with. Some secondary schools teach courses on preparation for marriage, but who teaches preparation for divorce? Newly divorced people often enter singlehood saddled with self-talk scripts guaranteed to make the transition needlessly painful. A host of irrational thoughts are born in the crucible of a failed marriage — ruminations over issues such as loneliness, a bleak future, and diminished self-worth.

Loneliness is a problem that is poorly understood by both divorced and single people. A newly divorced person is faced with large chunks of time spent alone, perhaps for the

> Loneliness is a problem that is poorly understood by both divorced and single people.

first time in years. Unless one's self-talk is rational, one may easily use this solitude to bring on powerful feelings of loneliness.

When I speak of *feelings* of loneliness, I'm being sloppy with language. True, most people think of loneliness as a feeling, but this is only partially accurate. Loneliness is a combination of two things: something objective and something subjective. The observable, objective reality is one's aloneness. When you're alone, it is not something in your head, it's an inescapable fact. A camera check would clearly show you sitting at home by yourself.

The second element in loneliness, the subjective dimension, is the cluster of thoughts you have **about** your aloneness. In other words, it's an evaluation of your physical state.

This rating of your physical state is often concealed through the use of half-sentences. For example: *I am alone...* (and it's horrible). Or, *I am alone...* (and I can't stand it). Or perhaps, *I am alone...* (and I shouldn't be). An inveterate whiner's thought might be, *I am alone...* (and it's not fair).

None of these added-on thoughts correspond to anything in the objective world. A camera check would show you were alone, but it would not show horribleness. It would not show you dying. And it would not show unfairness.

Aloneness does not equal loneliness. Nor does it equal horribleness or unbearableness or unfairness. And never forget: aloneness does not equal unworthiness. Avoid these unprovable equations. If you feel depressed when sitting at home on Saturday night, remember that your depression is not a result of your aloneness, it's a result of the thoughts you superimpose on a simple physical fact.

Aloneness does not equal loneliness.

Enough of theory. Let's look at some practical ways to combat loneliness. The first step is to uncover the poppycock in your self-talk. Start by making a three-column chart. In the first column, list all the thoughts you've been having about being alone. In the second column, write a response to each thought. If it's a rational thought, write, *This is a rational thought because...* If it's an irrational thought, write, *This is an irrational thought because...* In the third column, write rational sentences to replace all the nutty sentences you find in the first column.

This third column will become your new script. Copy it on a recipe card, and carry it with you. Go over it repeatedly until you've memorized it. Learn it so well you can recite it in your sleep backwards. Etch it so deeply in the tracks of your brain, you'll remember it even if you become catatonic.

Another excellent way to combat loneliness is to keep a day journal. Use it to record your thoughts, your questions, your doubts, your fears, your sadness. Be especially diligent in recording thoughts you have about planned solitary activities. Record how you feel about doing them alone. State whether you think you'll enjoy yourself. Try to express how much you think you'll enjoy yourself. Immediately after the experience, record how it went. Compare your expectations with what actually happened.

This will give you an ongoing record of your progress. If you keep exceeding your expectations, you'll know you're making progress with your self-talk. This, in turn, will enable you to build pride in your self-counselling skills.

Writing a journal can be an enriching experience. And please take notice: keeping a journal is something you do alone. Sometimes we fail to take note of how many rewarding things we actually do alone. For example, you surely prefer to read a book alone. And how about correspondence? Have you lost the habit? I correspond with many friends and relatives. This means I receive a lot of personal mail, both postal mail and email. Don't you enjoy finding personal letters in your mailbox? How about puttering with plants? If you have pets, I'm sure you enjoy playing with them. Have you ever tried painting or photography? These are rewarding hobbies most people prefer to do alone.

Lonely people need to make themselves aware of the personal enrichment that can happen while doing certain things alone. Here's a personal example. I joined the Sierra Club and made it my custom to hike twice weekly with a local chapter. One day I felt a strong urge to be in the mountains, but there was no hike scheduled by the club. I thought *what the heck* and went alone. What a revelation! I had never felt such joy on a hike. I saw and heard more birds. I saw and smelled more flowers. I saw far more wild animals, creatures that would have been frightened away by the noise of a chattering bunch of hikers.

Being alone gave me much greater freedom. I was able to leave beaten paths and explore at random. I discovered gorgeous waterfalls, limpid mountain pools, and quiet meadows with grazing deer, places I had unknowingly passed while hiking with the club. I discovered the pleasure of languidly eating lunch and taking a nap. Once I awoke to find a deer fawn standing over me, staring at this strange being — no doubt as curious as I was enchanted by the experience. In short, I communed with the wilderness as never before. I came to truly prefer hiking alone, although I still occasionally hiked with the club.

Suppose I had gone hiking alone and depressed myself with whining and horribilizing. I would have blinded myself to the beauty around me. You see, feelings of loneliness often come from the familiar problem of faulty focus. You can focus on *how well* you're doing, or you can focus on *what* you're doing. If, because you're alone, you see yourself as unwanted, rejected, and somehow failing, you can sabotage an otherwise joyful experience. If you choose to ignore the fact you're hiking alone and attend to the sounds and sights of the wilderness, you can have a deeply rewarding experience — one that may actually be enhanced because you're alone! Understand this, and you will be well on your way to becoming an independent person.

Many people seem to have the odd idea that to be independent is to be cold, uncaring, and somehow antisocial. What nonsense. Independent people simply use different self-talk when they're alone. Actually, independent people are more capable of genuine love and affection than neurotically dependent people. A dependent person tends to stew in his own anxiety. Despite her efforts to be outgoing and sociable, Clingy Cleo is actually self-centred. She's not really oriented toward others.

You will note that independent people are gracefully undemanding of others, while dependent people often are whiney and clinging. So don't believe for a moment you'll be seen as aloof or cold if you become more independent. The fact is you'll gain in social skills and likeability.

Independent people are prepared to let go of others when the time comes. They do this readily once they see a relationship is over. They're able to cut loose without bitter feelings. On the contrary, they treasure the good times they've spent with their partner.

Do you remember how you felt while reading a great book? Even though the book was long — perhaps a saga such as *War and Peace* — you didn't want it to end. When you finally turned the last page, you felt both joyful and sad, joyful for the beauty of the experience, but sad because it was over. It was time to return the book to the library, and you did so with no regrets. You felt enriched by your experience, and you looked to the future with anticipation. There were, after all, other great books to be read and enjoyed.

The fact that a book must end does not negate what you've experienced. Have you ever travelled to visit an old friend, spent long days together, reminisced endlessly, and then had to leave? Do you remember your final misty-eyed hug and the lump in your throat? Would you give up such a warmly fulfilling visit because you felt sad over parting?

The end of such an experience is sad, but it also can have warmth and beauty. Do you remember this lovely song made popular by Ray Price? The words are truly beautiful:

> Don't look so sad; I know it's over,
> But life goes on, and this old world will keep on turning.
> Let's just be glad we had some time to spend together.
> There's no need to watch the bridges that we're burning.
> Lay your head upon my pillow,
> Hold your warm and tender body close to mine,
> And make believe you love me one more time
> For the good times.

The title of this classic song refers to the attitude of two parting lovers as they make love just once more, *for the good times*. I'm sure this song has left more than one person misty eyed. But this sadness is mellowed by warm memories and gratitude. In a way, the singer cherishes his sadness. His acceptance that the affair is over enables him to feel nostalgia, not depression. It is this acceptance that is the crucial difference between nostalgia and depression.

An independent person feels nostalgic over loss, but he actively goes on with his life. A dependent person becomes depressed and immobilized. An independent person accepts loss; a dependent person whines over the 'unfairness' of his loss. The critical insight here is that acceptance of loss limits one's bad feelings to those of sadness, while non-acceptance of loss leads directly to the paralysis and pain of depression.

What type of person would you choose for a spouse or lover? Think about which of the following courtships would be most flattering: (1) you are courted by somebody who is enchanted by your intelligence, your ethical values, and your sensuality, or (2) you are cultivated by somebody who desperately 'needs' to have a lover.

Which person would be a better mate? The answer seems obvious, but many people actually gravitate toward dependent types. Why? Probably because they feel insecure with anybody who doesn't seem to 'need' them. Keep in mind that it is the independent person who is better equipped to become a loving and loyal partner.

Do you see now how neediness can undermine a love relationship? Think about it hard. And then think about it some more. Understanding this may one day save your love life.

Dependent people are good at playing the *addition game*. They do this by habitually adding subjective elements to real problems. If you're old enough, you may remember the television show *Dragnet*. Sergeant Joe Friday of the L.A. Police would interview an endless parade of witnesses. They always seemed to be exceptionally verbose, and they would embellish objective reality with horribilizing, should-ing, and all sorts of moral judgments. Sergeant Friday was continually interrupting these gabby characters with his famous plea, 'Just the facts, ma'am, just the facts.' These long-winded persons were actually highly believable. We all find it easy to believe our additions really describe things in the world as they objectively exist.

When people mentally play the addition game, their self-talk goes something like this:

Fact	Addition
I'm alone tonight.	This is awful.
Mary said I looked tired.	Mary was putting me down.
I don't have a lover.	It's not fair.
Phil rejected me.	Phil is a rotten person.

Are you beginning to see how subjective thoughts can lead to bad feelings when you superimpose them on real problems? To deepen your understanding, try playing devil's advocate. Make an effort to deliberately write some neurotic scripts. Write a cluster of thoughts that would make you feel depressed. Then write a script that would lead to anxiety and another that would generate anger. Make sure you include at least four thoughts in each script. Use your own language. This will help you get in touch with some of your hidden thoughts, distortional self-talk you commonly relay to Dummibrain.

As you uncover some of your nuttier thoughts, you may find it useful to develop some acronyms. One of my support group members used to talk about her I-NOTs (I-Need-Others Thinking). I thought this was creative because it implied extinguishing one's own growth while seeking the approval of others. Another member spoke of her ICSITs (I-Can't-Stand-It Thinking). Don't go overboard and drown in alphabet soup. An occasional acronym, however, can be a handy way to label a whole cluster of irrational thoughts with one word. And, of course, don't forget to use phrases such as *the Jehovah complex*, *the blame game*, and *I can'tism*.

Remember *I-can'tism*? This malady is endemic among singles. How often I've heard the words, 'I just can't find anybody.' This notion is often based on bogus evidence. Take Hapless Harry. He rarely spends time in an environment where he might meet a woman. His insecurity, pessimism, and self-downing saddle him with do-nothing behaviour. Most evenings, Harry sits at home watching baseball or B movies. When he ventures out, it's only to the corner tavern where he plays pool with his buddies. Since he rarely meets any women this way, he seldom dates or gets romantically involved.

Harry uses this lack of success as evidence that he can't meet a woman. He carries an all-too-common *non sequitur* in his head: *I'm not doing it now; so that proves I can't*. Of course, this only proves he's not doing it *now*. Watch out for this kind of *I can't*. If you find one in your self-talk change it to *I'm not doing it **now***. Or better yet, *I haven't succeeded in doing it so far*.

Next, remind yourself that events occur only when all the necessary prerequisites have been fulfilled. Then, and only then, will an event occur. If you withhold or fail to trigger any of the prerequisites, you'll prevent an event from happening. Put bluntly, the world is not crapping on you — you're crapping on yourself.

People often do things to themselves and then scream about how unfairly the world treats them. Keep reminding yourself that you must do what is necessary to make an event happen if you want it to happen. If you want a clean house, you must do what is necessary to make it a clean house. If you want to meet new people, you must do what is necessary to meet new people. And if you want a college degree, you must do what is necessary to get a degree.

Do you wince at how obvious this is? Believe me, this blatant truth is ignored by millions. In fact, I'll bet you've often ignored this simple fact. Be careful not to underestimate your potential for irrational thinking. I know that just when I think I'm becoming fairly rational, I seem to discover new non-sequiturs in my thinking.

Learning to think rationally in our neurotic society is a long-term project. It's also hard work. Don't kid yourself. Accept it as a probability that your thinking is laced with irrationalities. (Just make sure you simultaneously stress your human fallibility.)

Having stressed what is obvious, I now want to focus on one of the covert truths regarding fears of loneliness. If you dread being alone, you create an insidious form of self-oppression: *you make yourself a slave to your environment.* You demand and require that you have only surroundings that include other people. Nor is this all. These people must in some way focus on you. If you don't have this kind of peopled environment, you feel lonely, anxious and depressed. These feelings, in turn, are evidence that you *can't stand to be alone.* Do you see how this is a self-imposed servitude, a kind of slavery to a narrowly defined milieu?

I know of no writer who understood this kind of slavery more deeply than Thoreau. Have you read *Walden*? If you haven't read this great journal by Henry David Thoreau, I urge you to do so. He offers some compelling insights into the countless ways we enslave ourselves in modern society.

Another covert way we circumscribe our freedom is, paradoxically, through our refusal to recognize our limitations. If I understand, for example, that I cannot control the laws of the universe, I free myself to work for what is attainable. Knowing that I cannot read other people's minds frees me to better understand other human beings. If I realize that I cannot control others, I'm freed of shackles that block me from better control of my own emotions.

All this may seem rather disconnected, so let me expand my last example. If I know I can only **influence** others, I can more wisely provide behaviours for others to respond to. I'm free to use my wits to create things that others can choose to react to (or not react to). Do I stretch the meaning of freedom? Perhaps. But I see all irrational beliefs about others and ourselves as shackles. To break these bonds is to enlarge our true freedom. As a rule of thumb, whenever we choose to operate within the realm of the possible, we actually enlarge our possibilities.

One fiercely individualistic member of a support group rejected the notion that she could truly influence others. She asserted, 'I'm too deeply alienated to be able to relate to others. I feel a deep gulf between myself and any group I happen to be in.'

Alienation has been an ubiquitous concept in the psychobabble of our epoch. The locution *feelings of alienation* bombards us in modern pop psychology. But what does it mean? The word *alienation* is rich in connotation, but obscure in denotation. The word suggests and evokes more than it says; nonetheless, much importance is attached to this notion in modern thought. With this in mind, I want to pause to analyze this slippery term.

The phrase *feelings of alienation* is itself misleading. This is clearly not a feeling; it's a cluster of thoughts, a self-talk script. For example, people who report having this 'feeling' are in the habit of telling themselves they're profoundly different from the other members of their group, whatever group that might be.

This difference may be objectively real. Suppose you were a vegetarian homosexual atheist. You would have a world view and lifestyle that was notably different from the views and lifestyles of most Britons. So seeing yourself as different in some ways would be quite rational.

It would be useful to give this fact a label, so let's call it *differentiation* to distinguish it from alienation. This distinction is useful because the term alienation connotes a deep incompatibility between the alienated individual and society. It also seems to connote feelings of bitterness and depression; however, when you *differentiate* yourself from others you still see others as possible friends. In the case of alienation, you tend to see many groups and individuals as hostile. Most members of mainstream society may be seen as your enemies.

These semantic explorations are rather vague, so let's be more concrete. Imagine you're at a party. You're a gay secular humanist. Most of the people at the party are straight and go to church on Sundays. It doesn't take you long to realize you are different in significant ways from the other guests.

This is a critical moment. If you're merely disappointed because there aren't more people like you at the party, you'll simply feel regretful or mildly displeased. Given those mild feelings, you'll still be able to join the party and socialize. Let's assume you enter into conversation with a small group in one corner of the room. Assume you find yourself pulled into a lively discussion about films, a discussion you enjoy because you are a lifelong film buff with considerable knowledge about filmmaking.

One thing leads to another. You become the centre of attention as two other film buffs pepper you with questions. You discover that the two aficionados share your enthusiasm for French suspense films. They invite you to share a private showing of a classic French masterpiece the following weekend.

Now let's suppose you had started horribilizing when you first realized how different you were from the other guests. Suppose you had thought things such as *Horse manure! I don't think I can stand a whole evening with a bunch of pious breeders. They're probably all bigots. Why do there have to be so many bigots in the world?* Suppose you capped off your script with *I think I'll go sit by myself in the patio and give them all the cold shoulder.* That would be an example of alienation and then some.

Do you see the difference between the two scenarios? In the first scene, you merely recognized your difference from the others. In the second scene, you added an element of anger. The big difference, of course, lies in the two self-talk scripts.

The word alienation has its uses, but I urge you to avoid using it when describing yourself. The concept is overused, and it can distort your view of yourself and others. It tends to suggest that other people are your enemies when that usually is not the case. Sure, it's possible. But my experience is that people who talk about feelings of alienation are mind-reading, exaggerating, horribilizing, should-ing, condemning and so forth. They usually are not *being* alienated, they are alienating themselves.

Perceiving yourself as alienated is rarely justified by the facts. Yes, objective reality can be such that one would rationally see oneself as alienated. I recall a bizarre scene from a Richard

> **Perceiving yourself as alienated is rarely justified by the facts.**

Pryor movie that illustrates this possibility. Pryor, who is black, is walking through the woods one dark night when he suddenly finds himself marching in the middle of a hooded, torch-carrying Ku Klux Klan procession.

Who would argue with this hapless man if he later reported he had felt alienated? One of the most prominent thoughts of alienation is *I am in a hostile environment*. In the case of the Richard Pryor character, such a thought would surely be reasonable. But let's face it; alienation thoughts usually occur in social situations where there is no actual danger or deep hostility.

Ironically, some people generate anxious feelings and then use these feelings as proof they're in a hostile environment. Take the example of Fearful Fran. She was recently divorced and is exploring the singles scene. Fran is what Dr Albert Ellis calls a 'love slob'. Like all love slobs, Fran believes she *must* have a man, and it will be absolutely *horrible* if she doesn't find one. If we could eavesdrop on her thoughts, they would sound something like this: *I've just got to find somebody. Life without a man would be horrible. I just couldn't cope with the loneliness. Suppose I don't find somebody. Oh, God! The thought is just too horrible to bear.*

As you might guess, this script gets Dummibrain stirred up. He pulls Fran's panic levers and floods her with anxiety. Now comes the weird part. Fran has managed to manufacture what she thinks is evidence supporting her dotty thinking. She focuses on her anxiety and thinks, *I feel scared. My stomach is always in knots. Sometimes I feel shaky. I never felt like this when I was married. It just goes to show how much I need a man in my life.*

This generating of bogus evidence to support batty ideas is common. I once dated a talented and beautiful, albeit somewhat irrational, artist. On one of our first dates, we visited a famous waterfall and spent the afternoon hiking along a lovely brook. The following day, I met her for lunch. She was quite peevish with me. I was surprised and asked her what was wrong. She angrily said I had tried to hurt her during our hike. Perplexed, I asked what evidence she had for her belief. She thought about this for a long time. Then, with a frustrated shrug, she said, 'Well, I can't think of anything, but you must have tried to hurt me. Why else would I feel so angry toward you?'

This may sound preposterous, but it's an absolutely true story, and it reflects a common practice. Some people create bad feelings and then use the bad feelings as evidence that something bad has happened to them. Fran and my artist friend are alike in being highly dependent on the behaviour of others. Whether the behaviour is real or imagined doesn't matter to these women. Their emotional well-being is tethered to the vagaries of other people's actions, both real and fantasized.

A word of caution about the merits of dependency versus the merits of independence. We associate the word *independent* with being strong, resourceful, self-sufficient. Some people stretch it even further, so that it means good, meritorious, worthy. *Dependent*, on the other hand, is stretched to mean weak, bad, unworthy. If you buy this nonsense, you are slipping into an all-or-nothing fallacy.

Healthy independence doesn't mean going off and living in a cave, forsaking all human companionship, rejecting the amenities of civilization, and so forth. Along with the enjoyment and psychological benefits we derive from socializing, we depend on others for many things. As social animals, we often pool our skills and materials. We're not made weak by this pooling and interacting, we're made more powerful.

Consider my friends Bob and Judy. They personally built their entire house from the ground up. They repair their own cars, grow their own vegetables, raise their own poultry, make clothing for their children, make their own pottery, and so forth. They're the most self-sufficient people I know. But guess what: even they don't fix their own teeth. As a matter of fact, even dentists don't go so far as to fill their own cavities.

Asking others for help doesn't make you weak, vulnerable, or unfit. Social Darwinists see society as an arena of competition where only the fittest survive. The 'fittest', of course, meaning the 'best'. This is poppycock. Steer your thoughts away from these political views about worthiness and unworthiness.

> Asking others for help doesn't make you weak, vulnerable, or unfit.

Review Chapter 2 if this issue seems to be lurking in your scripts. Don't let irrational fears of dependency or vulnerability carry you to extremes in the other direction. Aim for a golden mean as you work to overcome your neediness and become an independent person. When I hear somebody brag, 'I don't need anybody', I tend to think, 'This person doth protest too much.'

A final caution. Your written work is highly important. Keep working on rewriting your self-talk scripts. Be relentless in purging the self-rating, horribilizing, demandingness, and neediness from your old scripts. Keep up your day journal, and record your progress.

Set up a reward-and-penalty system. Give yourself a reward every time you rewrite an old script. If you fail to do any written work whatsoever for 24 hours, penalize yourself. Write at least one script daily. Soon you'll be able to do new scripts easily and quickly in your head.

I've included a sample of how one goes about challenging an irrational script. You can do this in three columns if you prefer (see page 84). Some people split the challenges and the rational alternatives into two columns. I like the two-column system because I find that my alternative thoughts and my challenges overlap considerably. Try both methods. Then use the one you like best.

I also have included samples of three journal entries. A day journal is a highly personal thing; so tailor it to suit your needs. Just make sure you include some thinking about your thinking. If you're single and having problems with loneliness, be sure to do enjoyment-level predictions about any planned solitary activities.

Sample journal entries

San Diego, California
July 4, 2003 – 10 am.
I woke up feeling blue today. I was thinking about the 4th of July celebrations down at the beach. I wanted to go, but I didn't think it would be any fun without Jane. I knew right away my depressed feeling was coming from awfulizing about my going alone. I fought the notion that it would be awful and decided to force myself to go. I told myself that not having somebody to share the fun with was an inconvenience, not a disaster.

I'm making this entry now so I can predict my level of enjoyment. On a scale of one to ten, I figure my pleasure won't go over four.

July 4, 2003 – 11 pm.
I went to Ocean Beach for the festivities today. Four blocks were roped off. Two bands were playing, people were dancing in the streets, kids were dancing on roller skates. One band was playing memory tunes. I listened for an hour.

After that, I wandered over to the mechanical bull. People were lined up waiting for a chance to get thrown off. I found myself smiling as I watched people being tossed off and landing every which way. I watched this show for another hour.

By then I was hungry. I went to an outdoor café and ordered a spicy vegetable mash called falafel. It was really tasty! I'm sure I'll be trying it again.

Toward evening, I wandered along the cliffs and watched the sunset. This was the hardest moment. I missed Jane terribly. I ached to have her at my side sharing that beautiful moment. It was a spectacular sunset: purples, pinks and lavenders draped themselves over startling cloud formations.

Sample journal entries continued

I stayed on the cliffs to watch the fireworks. A large crowd gathered, and everybody was laughing and singing. The couple next to me began chatting with me. At the end of the fireworks, they asked me to dinner next Saturday. Seems they want me to meet a lady friend of theirs.

So how do I rate my day? I did feel lonely at times, but on the whole I enjoyed myself more than I had expected. I'd give my day at least a seven. Live music, amusing sights, delicious food, colourful fireworks, new friends, and a future dinner date. Yes, I'd say it definitely rated at least a seven. Certainly not my original four.

My worst moment was watching the sunset. I started out rationally missing Jane. The trouble is I kept inflating my thoughts. I got into horribilizing, dumping on myself, condemning Jane, and so forth.

I caught myself whining about how poorly I was coping with the loss of Jane. I challenged this by telling myself I was coping, albeit rather poorly. In other words, I was standing it; I just wasn't standing it as well as I wanted to. I guess I was demanding I do better than what I was doing. It's amazing how crazy my thinking gets sometimes. Tomorrow I'm going to write a rational sunset-watching script. The next time I'm having a beautiful experience, I'm going to have some saner self-talk to use. Maybe I'll always prefer to watch a sunset with a lover, but thinking I must have a lover to share it with is definitely nonsense.

July 5, 2003.
I reviewed the nutty script I was using yesterday. These thoughts seem to have been the main culprits:

My irrational thoughts

1. It's horrible to be without Jane.

2. I can't cope with the loss.

3. Jane never should have rejected me.

4. There's something wrong with me that caused me to ruin my relationship with Jane.

My four challenges

1. Horribleness doesn't exist. Being without Jane is an inconvenience, not a horror.

2. Obviously false. I would be dead if this were true. I simply am not doing as well as I prefer. I'll do better as I work on my self-counselling.

3. Nonsense. She **should** have rejected me. Her rejection of me didn't come out of a vacuum. All the prerequisites for her decision had to have been present for it to happen.

4. Maybe I made some bad mistakes, but that doesn't make me bad or a failure. If I fail at one thing, it doesn't mean my total personhood has failed. It only shows I'm a fallible human being.

EXAGGERATIONS   SHOULDS

NEEDINESS

I CAN'TISM   HORRIBLENESS

Witch's brew

Thoughts

1. I wish John would call me more often.

2. Why doesn't he call more often?

3. It's horrible when I don't hear from him.

4. I can't stand the waiting and wondering.

5. He shouldn't be so forgetful. He should be more considerate of my feelings.

6. His lack of respect shows he doesn't care for me.

7. I feel like he's putting me down.

8. How can he be so cruel?

9. I'm not going to call him anymore and see how he likes it.

10. That'll teach him!

Challenges and alternatives

1. This is a rational thought. My wish is a fact.

2. A rhetorical question meaning he should call me more often. But what law says he should act the way I prefer? Scientifically speaking, he should do exactly as he does.

3. False. Horribleness is mythical. It doesn't exist objectively. I'm adding to reality.

4. False. I'm standing it at this very moment. It's true I would prefer to stand it better, but I am standing it.

5. False. If he's forgetful, he should be forgetful. If he's inconsiderate, he should be inconsiderate.

6. I'm trying to read his mind. I can't possibly read his thoughts. People who try to read minds usually botch it.

7. False. I don't **feel** it — I **think** it. His acts can't possibly diminish me. I'm worrying about a mythical self-worth.

8. A rhetorical question. The answer is easily. Furthermore, cruel is a subjective notion. He doesn't think his behaviour is cruel.

9. I want to punish him because I irrationally equate him with one 'bad' behaviour and condemn his entire personhood.

10. Nonsense. He may change his behaviour, but probably not for the better.

6

I'll Starve Myself Tomorrow

> ❝ If a chicken followed the advice that he should not peck unless he pecked accurately at all times, he would simply starve to death. ❞
>
> Paul Hauck

Procrastination is an emotional problem. Yes, that's right. If you habitually procrastinate, you're in the grip of disturbed thinking. I'm aware that the dictionary says something like *Reprehensibly putting off until tomorrow what should be done today.* Admittedly, this doesn't sound all that bad. But remember what we learned in Chapter 1: dictionaries only give us equivalent words, expressions that still fail to tell us what a thing *is.* Accordingly, we had best try for a deeper analysis of this habit of dallying and goofing off, a behaviour that can painfully handicap our lives.

First, I want to make it clear that not all putting off is self-defeating. On the contrary, rationally setting priorities is in our best interest. When I set priorities, I merely order tasks according to their importance or in ways that are beneficial to me. When I procrastinate, I escape from doing tasks I've promised myself I would do. I made such a pledge because I believed a completion of those activities would be good for me in the long run.

Let's be honest about this. If you make a promise to yourself to do X because X is in your best interest, and then you weasel out of doing it, you're being self-destructive. Surely you know that sabotaging one's own goals is a characteristic of neurosis. So let me say it again: *procrastination is an emotional problem*.

So why do we do it? The answer is complicated. The nutty thinking behind procrastination is more jumbled than most people realize. Humans have spent thousands of years inventing every trick imaginable to get out of doing what's in their best interest to do. The number of cop-outs we use in our self-talk seems endless. We have the ability to create an amazing labyrinth of self-deception.

Nonetheless, we can use broad brush strokes and reduce the causes of procrastination to a few underlying beliefs. In Chapter 2 we saw a major cause, the ubiquitous belief in self-worth. The inordinate fear of losing this mythical thingamajig feeds much, if not most, procrastination. As I've pointed out, the fear of making mistakes and being diminished makes a person fearful of treading new pathways. If you're in the habit of laying your ego on the line every time you try a new experience or tackle a new skill, you'll feel inclined to delay, set back, postpone, embog, impede, derail, block, and hinder every new project. If you put your self-worth up for grabs, you will feel constrained to dawdle, dally, drag, lag, loiter and poke. The stakes are simply too high to take the plunge.

The malignancy of self-rating underlies this suffocating timidity. If you're a procrastinator, there's a good chance you're rating your whole personhood on the basis of your

> The malignancy of self-rating underlies this suffocating timidity.

performances. As I noted in Chapter 2, this works fine when you're performing well. Alas, we fallible human beings don't always perform well. We all have bad days when we burn the toast, misplace our car keys, miss a freeway exit, write the wrong date on a cheque, forget our own phone number. Think about what happens if you put your personal value on the line every time you make a mistake. Won't you feel continually stressed?

Ironically, much of this stress comes from botching simple, well-learned tasks. Even when doing the most automatic behaviour, you can easily goof and thereby expose your unworthiness. Presto! You magically go from a highly capable person to a bungling fool. What an awful thought! How can you even contemplate trying something new?

Many timid souls forget that a defining characteristic of learning is the making of mistakes. If you aren't making mistakes while learning X, you're not **learning** how to do X — you are **doing** X. In other words, if you do something perfectly, you obviously know how to do it. Would you take tennis lessons if you were able to step on the court for the first time and play a perfect game? I repeat: if you aren't making mistakes, you're not learning how to do something, you are doing it.

Are you beginning to see what a bummer it is to believe in the myth of self-worth? This irrational belief can affect everything you do in life. Think about how seriously it can impair your growth. If learning means making mistakes, and if mistakes are seen as magically shining a spotlight on your absolute unworthiness, such a myth can drastically curtail your growth.

Better to delay doing X. After all, you're not ready to let the world know what an incompetent no-goodnik you are. Maybe if you stall you can avoid the risk. Maybe you can reach your goals another way. Better to simply dawdle until you figure out a risk-free way to get what you want. In the end, of course, you seldom achieve what you desire.

This cowardly stalling entangles you in a classic cycle of self-downing and procrastination. You easily see that your reasons for not doing X are flimsy. Knowing this, you dump on yourself. Then, as you give yourself a low rating, you're more likely to see X as too hard to attempt. Then you ask yourself something like *How can a weak person like me ever do X successfully?* The result is still more stalling.

Years ago, Dr Herdie Baisden, a fine rational counsellor and key mentor of mine, once described to me what he called *the cycle of self-hate and procrastination.* He divided this cycle into four cognitive steps:

1. I know it would be better for me to do X, but I generally don't do well at such things, and I might fail. If I fail, then everyone will know how inferior I really am.
2. I'd better delay doing X. I don't want others to see how hopeless I really am.
3. See! Just look at me. See how I drift and wallow. I'm too weak and irresponsible to ever get anywhere in life. My constant idling proves how worthless I am.
4. Now I know I can't ever do X, so why should I try?

Dr Baisden diagramed this cycle thus:

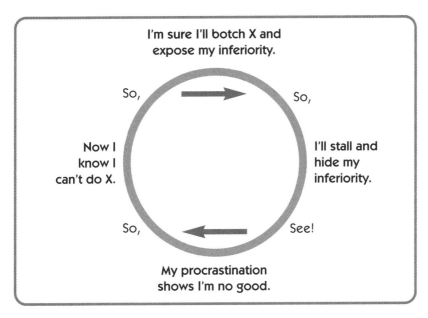

Notice how step four merges with step one as you lock yourself into a destructive cycle of self-hate and procrastination. Do you recognize this cycle in yourself? If so, I urge you to revisit Chapter 2. You need to build up a confidence that you can tolerate your inevitable mistakes and the disapproval of others. Review the sample scripts in Chapter 2. Write some of your own. Energetically attack any tendencies to globally rate yourself rather than your performances. If you learn to focus on what you're doing and not on how well you are doing, you will eliminate a major source of procrastination.

Another potent ally of procrastination is a poor tolerance of frustration. We are often thwarted from getting what we want. Even if we are not completely blocked, we often find that getting what we want requires hard work and considerable discomfort. In other words, we bump into frustrations. To repeat what I said in Chapter 4, frustration is not a feeling — it is something that blocks us from getting our way. So-called feelings of frustration are feelings generated by how we look at actual frustrations. Depending on the script being used, the emotion can be anger, anxiety, or depression. Keep this distinction in mind. It will help you stay problem-centred, rather than self-centred.

When you run up against a frustration, that is problem number one. If you upset yourself over the frustration, that is problem number two, a problem you have created. If you manage to focus solely on how to overcome the frustration, you will find you can work more calmly and reflectively. In short, you will reap the benefits of staying problem-centred. Or, if you choose, you can wallow in an emotional stew concocted by your misdirected self-talk.

Inability to handle frustration is often called *low frustration tolerance* (LFT). This common trait is closely tied to the Jehovah complex. This linkage occurs because some of us foolishly believe our frustrations should not exist. If you want to overcome procrastination, work hard on your acceptance of reality. Review Chapter 4 and work on your anti-should-ing scripts. Once you convince yourself your frustrations should exist, you will be better prepared to deal with them.

On the other hand, if you believe life should be easy, that you should never be thwarted, that others should act as you demand, and that the world should be fair, you will find yourself obsessively dwelling on the 'horribleness' of life's endless frustrations. Alas, this very obsession will become another frustration blocking you from getting what you want.

Face reality. If X is hard to do, if it means getting sweaty or dirty, if it means missing your favourite TV show, if it's unpleasant in any way, that's exactly the way it should be. When all the prerequisites are present, the discomfort of doing X must, should and will exist. What should happen will happen.

Many of us continue to crazily deny this. Take the case of Pokey Pete. He's been thinking about insulating his attic for five years. Pete knows the attic is hot, dirty, and painfully awkward to work in. So he tells himself, 'I don't feel like climbing into that hot, stuffy hole. I just don't feel sufficiently inspired. I think I'll wait until I feel more like doing it. After all, the attic has been without insulation since the house was built 50 years ago. A little longer won't hurt. It's not that important.'

So Pokey Pete waits and waits and waits. He waits for the day when he'll 'feel more like doing it'. Of course, the attic continues to be a hot, dirty, awkward place to work in. You see, that's really the problem. Pete is actually waiting for the conditions to change, not his mood. He'll never like working under those conditions. As a consequence, Pete is still waiting after five years.

In the meantime, his energy bills go higher and higher. This, in effect, reduces his income. As a result, Pete worries about the waste of money. Next, he rebukes himself for being irresponsible and for being lazy. Then he feels depressed. Or he may curse the utility company, the climate, and the party who sold him the house. Then he feels angry.

Oddly enough, Pete never stops to think about how uncomfortable these feelings and thoughts are, or about the discomfort of having less money to spend on personal pleasures. If Pete would sit down and think about it, he'd see that a single afternoon in the attic would be less uncomfortable than the ongoing mental hassles he's putting himself through.

Note the fallacy in Pete's self-talk. He pooh-poohs the importance of the job. True, it's not a life-or-death matter. The sun will still rise if Pete's attic remains

> **Note the fallacy in Pete's self-talk.**

uninsulated. But this is true of all the jobs Pete promises to do. So what? This is a blatant example of either-or thinking. Either it is all-important, or it has no importance. This hoary fallacy hardly deserves attention, so let's just call it baloney.

After all, Pete has already decided it's in his best interest to insulate his attic. He wants a warmer house, less draftiness, lower heating bills, an increase in his home equity, and the satisfaction of conserving energy; so the task clearly has importance. That issue is settled. A mental debate over the degree of importance usually is a delaying tactic that wastes time and energy.

Downgrading the importance of the job is a smoke screen to hide Pete's low frustration tolerance. Bear in mind that Pete's LFT is a subjective problem, not a physical one. At the edge of Pete's consciousness is a script he uses when facing disliked tasks. By now you may be able to guess how a typical progression of Pete's thoughts might evolve: (1) *That attic is a horrible place, and putting in insulation is a horrible job.* (2) *I can't stand working in hot, cramped places like that.* (3) *That damned attic should have been insulated years ago by the last owner. I shouldn't have to do it.*

Go over each of these thoughts. Underline the key irrational words. Can you see what is irrational in each belief? What rational thoughts can be used instead? Try to mentally compose a rational script regarding the insulating of a attic. Also think about an uncomfortable task you've been putting off. Try looking for any inflated thoughts about the job. Then replace them with thoughts that more accurately describe the job.

This probing has to be an ongoing enterprise if you want to be successful in your self-counselling. This is especially true regarding your LFT. This trait is often entangled in hidden philosophical notions. For example, the belief *things should go easily for me* implies a hidden Jehovah complex. Another issue lurking beneath LFT is that of short-range hedonism versus long-range hedonism. Do you want immediate pleasure? Or do you want long-range gratification?

Rational psychotherapy comes down on the side of long-range hedonism, a position I heartily endorse. I believe we should enjoy life as much as we can. Just remember that a long-range view of happiness usually works best. It's a question of present pleasure for future pain versus present pain for future pleasure. A corollary of this is the fact that future pleasure always seems to be richer and more enduring than present pleasure. I'm sure you're aware that immediate pleasures often are all too brief. They seldom offer deep and enduring satisfaction. A weekend spent watching football may be fun and relaxing, but it's not something you can savour for long.

Suppose you have the choice of spending the weekend watching four bowl games or painting your shabby, peeling garage. Let's say you choose to paint the garage. You spend time on Friday afternoon and Saturday morning scraping, sanding, and preparing. On Saturday afternoon, you apply a coat of paint. On Sunday, you apply the final coat.

Voilà! Your whole house and yard are enhanced by a shiny new garage. Each day when you come home from work, you stop for a moment and admire your handiwork. Each time you look at the garage, you feel a glow of satisfaction over a job well done. Furthermore, you no longer worry about wood rot or suffer the teasing of neighbours and friends. Best of all, you don't have to think about painting your garage for years to come.

Compare that satisfaction with the fun of watching a few football games. And think about how much more fun watching games will be from now on. During commercials, you can stare out the window and admire your shiny new garage. This is important to understand. Even your short-term pleasures are now enhanced. Through your 'sacrifice', you can now have your cake and eat it too.

This has another less obvious benefit: you have made a serious inroad into your habit of procrastinating. You will want to build on this. Look at the experience as corroborating evidence, a form of proof that such jobs are not too odious to bear. Remind yourself that you can actually stand missing football one weekend to do some allegedly horrible tasks. Reinforce this. Use self-talk such as: *See! That wasn't bad at all. It wasn't horrible, and it wasn't too hard. I certainly was able to stand it. What the heck, I even caught myself whistling while I worked. I'm going to remember this experience the next time I think something is **too** hard.*

Too is one of those words I label as magical. It is exceptionally vague, as magical words usually are. It seems to mean there's a point beyond which one is unwilling or unable to go in bearing

> *Too* is one of those words I label as magical.

discomfort. It implies one couldn't survive doing a disliked task. I suggest you prune such fuzzy terms from your self-talk. At best, they confuse your thinking. At worst, they incite Dummibrain to produce negative physical feelings. These feelings, in turn, only serve to make the *too hard* jobs even harder.

You see, we can actually make an easy job harder simply by the way we evaluate it. Pokey Pete does this. Sometimes the work piles up at his office. When the pile reaches a certain point, Pete sees the work as *too much*. This implies the work is more than he can finish or cope with. At that point, Pete catastrophizes and soon works himself into a state of anxiety. Rattled by his own anxiety, he doesn't focus on the problem or work to solve it. A couple of evenings or one Saturday afternoon at the office is all Pete needs to catch up. The solution is fairly easy, but Pete's anxiety-generating thoughts make it hard.

Related to the too much concept is an incantational *I can't*. Pete's *I-can'tism* is a sure path to immobilizing himself. He destroys his own motivation. 'Why try to do what I can't possibly do?' he asks himself. As if this weren't enough, Pete uses the infamous *double whammy* on himself. He first says, 'There's far

Dummibrain will take you at your word. If you link I can'tism with musturbation, you will goad him into hammering you with the dreaded double whammy.

too much to do. *I can't* possibly finish in time.' Secondly, he says, 'The deadline is next week, and *I have to* have the work done by then.' The formula looks like this: I can't + I have to = double whammy.

Have you ever used a double whammy on yourself? If you work at a job with deadlines, you probably have used this fearsome club to beat yourself. If not, you may have used it while Christmas shopping or preparing for an exam or getting ready for a trip. Many of us are rather creative about finding ways to use the gruesome double whammy.

Both thoughts in a double whammy need to be challenged and processed. The *must* statement, in particular, needs to be zeroed in on. *Musturbation* is at the core of most emotional disturbance; so give priority to locating your oughts, musts, and shoulds. Exile these tyrants. This will help put you back in touch with objective reality. If you're telling yourself, *I must have these reports finished by next week*, attack the must. Tell yourself, *I don't have to finish my work this week, or any week, for that matter. I can even choose to never finish it.* Do this and you will feel Dummibrain breathing a sigh of relief.

I've got to finish by Friday.

I gotta show I'm capable.

I must do it anyway.

Oh, what's the using of trying?

I can't possibly do it.

Not even Superman could do it.

But it's clearly impossible.

Pokey Pete clobbers himself with a double whammy.

Once you've uprooted your *musts*, and you feel relatively calm, you can start working at whatever task you are facing while motivating yourself in rational ways. While doing this, be sure to tell yourself it's in your best interest to either finish your reports by working a few extra hours or at least come close to finishing the job. You don't **have to** finish your reports, but you had best try to calmly and methodically finish them if you want that promotion you're working for.

Don't forget to periodically remind yourself of your long-term goals. Review what you have to do to reach each goal. Suppose you had the goal of learning desktop publishing so as to expand your computer skills. Ask yourself, *What* exactly *do I have to do to learn this skill?* By doing this, you'll be putting together a list of rational shoulds to motivate yourself. Use these in place of your old irrational shoulds. You don't have to work on learning a quota of desktop publishing skills every night, but you had best do a little each day to reach your goal.

By using irrational musts to motivate yourself, you may turn yourself into a rebel without a cause. A rebel without a cause first says, *I have to do X.* Then he bitterly thinks *I hate doing X. I don't want to do X. Why should I have to do X? I resent having to do X.* Of course, nobody is forcing him to do X. The rebel without a cause merely feels 'forced' because of his self-imposed must.

Another way to irrationally motivate yourself is through fear. Students are good at this. A student postpones studying for a test. Each day he thinks about how dangerously close the test is. He awfulizes about what will happen if he fails. Each day his anxiety builds. Finally, a day or two before the test, his anxiety level is so high he decides studying would be preferable to suffering such acute anxiety. He plunges into his studies, foregoing sleep, food, and recreation. In a crude way, the system works. The learning, however, is superficial, and much unnecessary stress is created.

You don't need fear to motivate yourself. Do you use fear to make yourself buckle your seat belt? Do you scare yourself into not eating food with known carcinogens? Do you use frightening thoughts about

> **You don't need fear to motivate yourself.**

cholesterol and heart attacks to make yourself go jogging? Do you imagine yourself splattered over the road to make yourself wait for a green light before crossing the street?

The fact is you do many things because you think it's in your best interest to do so. This proves you can rationally and calmly motivate yourself to do goal-oriented tasks, whether they are liked or disliked.

This involves both short- and long-term plans of action. Choose your long-range goals first. Then form a plan for reaching your goals. The plan you choose will, in effect, be a series of short-term decisions. These decisions are what procrastination threatens to undermine. Remember: your long-term goal will result from what you do today and tomorrow and the next day. It is a series of individual acts and decisions that culminate in taking you to a long-term goal.

So take things on a day-to-day basis. If you want to lose 50 pounds, focus on today's diet and exercise. Make it your goal to lose a fraction of a pound today. The fractions will eventually add up to 50 pounds.

> **So take things on a day-to-day basis.**

While reaching a long-term goal can be exciting, the daily choices and activities that carry you to your goal can often be rather uninspiring. This brings us to the problem of boredom. Boredom can easily lead to procrastination, so let's analyze it and see what we can do about it. Have you ever thought about what the word *boredom* means? Stop for a minute, and try to define what this condition is.

As you will see, boredom is a mystifying concept. I used to be puzzled when members of my support groups would complain about the boredom they were suffering at work or in their marriages. As I often do, I decided to follow the sound advice of Dr Albert Ellis and *cherchez le should*. Well, I didn't have to look far to find the first should. There it was, our old friend the Jehovah complex at the very centre of boredom. You see, at bottom, boredom is a form of demandingness, a demand that your environment entertain you.

Take the case of Irate Irene — a woman with a pronounced case of LFT. Irene works in an office and does routine clerical duties.

When at work, her self-talk sounds like this: *God, this is boring. How can anyone be expected to do such boring work day after day? There should be more variety and stimulation. I can't stand the tedium. It's so unfair. I deserve better than this. Life is a drag.*

As you might expect, Irene feels tense, fatigued, and angry. Actually, her work is easy to do and can be done with a minimum of discomfort. If Irene were using rational self-talk, she would feel relatively neutral toward her work. She might even focus on how to make it more interesting. She might find ways to be more efficient and productive. This could conceivably get the supervisor's attention, who might give her some more work, some of which might be more interesting. Of course, none of this will happen if Irene doesn't go to work on her flawed self-talk instead of focusing on her boredom.

Just as there is no law saying life must be fair, there is no law saying the world owes us entertainment. If you're like Irene, who demands that everything in life be interesting, you may procrastinate about washing the dishes, exercising, dieting, flossing your teeth, buying groceries, cleaning the house, getting medical checkups, and so forth — all of which are in your best interest to do.

People who spend the whole day watching soap operas and eating chocolate may be entertaining themselves, but doing so is hardly in their best interest. The fact is most of the things we do in our own best interest are not what one could call exciting. But if they aren't, then they aren't — and that's the way it should be. That is unless you're Jehovah, and you can command the way in which reality unfolds.

Demandingness and horribilizing are, at bottom, superstitious attitudes toward reality. Demandingness denies the cause-and-effect nature of reality. Horribilizing adds a subjective overlay to reality. We are interested in this added layer because it often is the starting point in triggering one's LFT. Pokey Pete continually uses negative exaggerations about jobs he has promised to do. What Pete needs is to do some anti-horribilizing in his self-talk.

This anti-horribilizing, however, may not be enough. We often are unconvinced by purely intellectual refutations of our nutty ideas. As you will recall, in Chapter 2 I suggested some shame-attacking exercises to support the refutation of the idea that disapproval diminishes a person. Once you suffer disapproval and see yourself unmarked by the event, you find it easier to abandon the screwy beliefs you have about needing approval. You will have collected evidence to support a new rational belief.

This same approach is useful for refuting exaggerations about disliked tasks. If Pokey Pete uses rational self-talk about the job of insulating his attic, it may not be enough. His old irrational ideas may still dominate, and he may need some hard evidence to be convinced. To get this proof, he will need to enter the hated attic and start laying insulation. At that point, he will see for himself that laying insulation is not 'horrible', and that he can easily stand the discomfort. The point is, Pete may have to push himself into the initial behaviour so as to breathe some life into his rational, but sometimes arid, self-counselling.

This experience can be buttressed with another technique I described in Chapter 5. As you will recall, I recommended keeping a day journal and making predictions of enjoyment levels for things you do alone. This was to be followed up with a second assessment of your enjoyment level following the experience. You can use this same tool when dealing with your LFT, except that you will be predicting discomfort levels.

Let's say Pete adopted this system. Let's further assume he thought about the job of insulating his attic and predicted a discomfort level of eight on a scale of one to ten. Suppose he was agreeably surprised by how easy it was and later recorded a discomfort level of only three. If Pete uses this tool consistently when tackling hateful jobs, the numbers will begin to have a healthy impact on Pete's overblown awfulizing. Numbers have a solid, tangible feel abut them. They give a person confidence that he or she is making real progress. In Pokey Pete's case, he would have a visible way to measure the progress he is making in raising his LFT. Who knows, perhaps one day he'll be able to boast he has achieved HFT (high frustration tolerance). Perhaps they'll even start calling him Pronto Pete!

To get Pete started in attacking his procrastination, I would encourage him to use what Dr Albert Ellis calls *The Five-Minute*

Plan. Under this scheme, Pete would contract with himself to spend at least five minutes working in the attic. At the end of five minutes, he would be free to contract with himself to spend five more minutes, and so forth. In any case, he's only obliged to do the original five minutes, never more.

Personally, I've found the Ellis plan to be the most effective anti-procrastination tool I've ever used. In fact, much of this book has been written using this five-minute contract. Writing is hard, solitary, tiring work. It is also highly frustrating if you type as badly as I do. My reluctance to sit down and start writing or proofing easily leads me to procrastinate. I find myself goofing off by listening to music, reading magazines, or playing chess on my computer.

To break out of this pattern, I simply make an agreement with myself to do at least five minutes of writing. I don't require that it be thought out or researched. In fact, I usually discard what I've written during those five minutes.

Nonetheless, those initial five minutes of writing almost always achieve their purpose: my inertia and dawdling are disrupted. Generally, that's all I need. You see, I feel far more positive about writing when I'm writing than when I'm not writing. Often when people ask me if I enjoy writing I may say, 'Hell no. It's tedious, lonely work. I wouldn't recommend it to anybody.' But when I'm actually writing, I don't think about these negatives. On the contrary, I usually get deeply absorbed in what I'm doing.

My problem is that I have two sets of ideas battling for supremacy: (1) *writing is too hard, too boring, and too lonely,* and (2) *writing is rewarding, absorbing, fascinating work.* The first ideas are irrational. Whenever they dominate, I have to challenge and disprove them by simply doing five minutes of writing.

After I started using the Ellis technique, I never again had so-called writer's block. Now I no longer believe there is such a thing. It's obvious a person can always write something, even if it's pure junk and ends up in the wastebasket. The point is that whatever mess you may have written, it proves you aren't blocked. Once your inertia is overcome, you will begin building momentum, a forward impetus that may start some of your best ideas flowing. Writer's block is merely a form of I-can'tism in the self-talk of writers. So if you owe letters to six people, use the five-minute plan each night for a week. You may be surprised by how far you go toward overcoming what we might label letter writer's block.

Correspondence with friends can be richly rewarding, but I believe it's an acquired taste, something that is true of many activities we try only a few times and then abandon. Some of the most dedicated runners say they hated running in the beginning. Some people hate opera the first time they see one, but they turn into rabid fans after further exposure. Many people hate lifting weights the first few weeks. Then, as the results begin to show, they become ardent bodybuilders.

So give yourself a chance to acquire new tastes. Take the time to adjust to new experiences. The initial discomfort usually passes as your skill and appreciation increase. If not, at least you will have increased your frustration tolerance — no small gain!

> So give yourself a chance to acquire new tastes.

I don't mean to suggest something like running will ever be easy. Any fool can see it's easier to plop down in an easy chair, enjoy some snacks, and read a pulp novel. Who would deny it?

Or is it so obvious? If it's really easier to not exercise, why is it that people who stay in good physical condition seem to be happier, less stressed, and more full of energy? Is it really easier to feel tired? To feel tense? To feel mentally lethargic? Is it easier to feel exhausted after walking up three flights of stairs? Is it easier to have more colds and flu? Is it easier to have heart disease and a weak back? Maybe we should rethink the obvious.

The belief that putting things off is easier than doing them now is a common delusion. This self-defeating crackpot idea is a major reason for procrastination. Attack it whenever it crops up in your thinking. When you are composing anti-procrastination scripts, always include the question, *Is it **really** easier to not do X?*

Relentlessly ask yourself: is it easier to be overweight, or is it easier to exercise? Is it easier to do the dishes after coming home from the theatre, or is it easier to do them now? Is it easier to work as a waitress for 30 years, or is it easier to do a vocational course for two years? Is it easier to have tooth decay, or is it easier to floss my teeth daily for two minutes? Is it easier to have heart disease, or is it easier to stop smoking? If nothing on this list applies to you, take a few minutes to make up a list of six such pairs. Then post it on your bathroom mirror.

Being clear about which path is easier requires a realistic view of how much time is needed. One way we sabotage our ability to tolerate tasks is by exaggerating the time they take. I recently found myself making this mistake. I have chronic lower-back pain, and my doctor tells me I need strong abdominal muscles to minimize my pain. I've found this to be true; so I do sit-ups every morning, a duty I heartily curse. This is especially true in the morning, when I'm stiff and half-asleep.

Over a period of time, I found myself skipping my sit-ups whenever I was in a hurry. Dimly aware that LFT was involved, I tuned in on my self-talk. One key thought was easy to locate — I was simply telling myself I didn't have time for my sit-ups.

To process this, I decided to be scientific. I went to a sporting goods store and bought an inexpensive stopwatch. The next morning I timed my sit-ups. To my amazement, it took only 70 seconds to do an unhurried 50 sit-ups. Through an irrational, unscientific, completely subjective judgment, I had concluded that I couldn't spare 70 seconds each morning to help prevent chronic back pain.

This experience intrigued me. I began thinking about the possible uses of a stopwatch in self-counselling. Soon I was timing all my daily duties. I was surprised at how quickly many thought-to-be tedious tasks are actually done. I found it took two minutes to floss my teeth. Scooping and freshening the cat's litter box took less than three minutes. Sweeping the kitchen floor took three minutes. Loading and unloading the dishwasher, doing the laundry, scrubbing sinks, and other menial tasks took far less time than I had subjectively estimated.

If you procrastinate, buy a stopwatch. Start timing every disliked household task. How long does it take to wrap and take out the garbage? How long does it take to check the air in your tyres?

How long does it take to write a cheque for your electric bill? How long does it take to scrub the toilet bowl? Record these times in your day journal. Use them to challenge your LFT.

This will make you feel foolish about your awfulizing. Avoiding or putting off a job will seem grossly irrational when you find it takes only 70 seconds or so. As a final caveat, if you could measure the time spent mentally procrastinating, you would feel even more foolish.

I'm talking about a simple fact: the objective world is often markedly different from our subjective world. Objective time is different from subjective time. It may seem like an eternity to you when you're doing an exercise. If so, use a stopwatch to measure the time it takes. Such measurements help you strip away the magical overlays we add to reality. Remember that getting your judgments closer to objective reality is at the very core of rational self-counselling.

As you hone and practise this skill, you will be undermining another skill: your talent for putting things off. Yes, procrastination is a kind of skill. And, like all skills, it requires practise. You see, each time you avoid doing what's in your best interest, you practise avoidance. I won't say practise makes perfect because you're a fallible human being who will never achieve perfection. But you can get very good at avoidance if you systematically practise it. If, for example, you consistently avoid meeting new people, you will become a skilled wallflower.

Consider Pokey Pete. He has been practising avoidance all his life. He has carried it to a fine art. His avoidance scripts are masterpieces of self-deception, faulty evidence, flawed logic, and plain old superstition. If Pete is at a party and he sees a woman he is attracted to, he easily and efficiently talks himself out of approaching her.

Pete slides into such thoughts as *Wow, would I like to meet her. I think I'll say something to her. Yeah, but what happens if she tells me to buzz off. What if she gives me an icy stare and says something like, 'Get lost, idiot.' Everybody would see me slinking off, completely humiliated. I definitely would come off as a real idiot. But, oh man, she sure is pretty. Gosh, she's actually smiling at me. I suppose she thinks I'm funny looking. No point in talking to her. I'd never have a chance anyway. Aw heck, maybe I'll try. Oops! Now she's talking to another guy. I better wait until she's alone.*

Just in the nick of time! Pete is reprieved from the horrible fate of talking to a strange woman and possibly being rejected. Whew. What a close call. Now Pete can relax and look for another woman to meet. Did I say 'meet'? I really should say '...another woman to *avoid* meeting.' Pete's forte is avoidance, not doing.

We have to give credit to Pete's energetic practising. Each time he stalls and avoids meeting a woman, he gets a little better at it. Remind yourself of this harsh fact whenever you use an avoidance script. Tell yourself *If I don't talk to this person, I'll be practising goal-defeating behaviour. If I stall or think I need time to build up my courage, I'm just kidding myself. The next time will always be harder. And the time after that will be harder still.*

I learned this early. As a teenager, my chosen sport was gymnastics. I learned that putting off new stunts only made them harder and riskier. The longer I stalled, the more I would crowd scary thoughts into my self-talk. Eventually my emotion-brain would have me so immobilized, I would tend to freeze in the middle of my attempt at a new stunt — a paralysis that clearly was not in my best interest. My greatest success in progressing to more advanced stunts came when I made the decision to try one and then acted before I could generate an avoidance script.

One of my experiences is a good illustration. When my high school gymnastic team put on its annual show before the school assembly, I was slated to do a high-bar routine. Just before I went on stage, I suddenly decided it was time for me to try the giant swing — a stunt I had never done before. I decided it was important to make a decision and then immediately do it; so I walked out on stage in front of 2,000 students and performed my first giant swing. Needless to say, my coach and teammates were flabbergasted. After my coach recovered from his surprise, he laughed gleefully at my nerve.

Make a decision, then act. Stalling only makes it harder the next time you try to act.

Make a decision, then act.

If I hadn't acted so quickly, I might have stalled for weeks or months. As it was, I made a breakthrough and soon progressed from class B gymnastics to class A. The point is you never move from class B to class A unless you *do* it. Remember: thinking about doing X is not doing X — thinking about X equals avoiding X.

If you're an avoider, start recording your postponements. Each time you think about doing something, but then postpone doing it, record your dawdling. At the end of the day, include these incidents in your day journal. Review your avoidance record weekly. As you become more aware of your procrastination patterns, you will begin to see an automatic drop in the number of times you shirk doing promised jobs. Research and clinical experience show that *mere awareness of an unwanted behaviour will reduce it.* What a wonderfully easy way to change behaviour! As you can see, your day journal is invaluable, not only as a record of what you do, but as a record of what you don't do.

Recording unwanted behaviour has another plus: it helps you to keep a rational perspective. Suppose you're on a diet. Each night you record in your journal the number of meals you have eaten that obey your dietary rules. Suppose that on the eleventh day you get upset over something and decide to stuff yourself. You devour a steak, baked potato with sour cream, pie à la mode, coffee with cream and sugar, and an after-dinner liqueur. Definitely a hearty meal. You'll have to admit you've stumbled on your way to losing weight.

Now suppose you make another common mistake: you fall into all-or-nothing thinking. You tell yourself, *Damn it, I really blew it. I completely undid my diet. I'm right back at square one. What's the use of trying? I never do anything right. I guess I'm just too weak and worthless to follow a simple diet.* Needless to say, Dummibrain starts pushing buttons right and left, and you are soon in an emotional stew.

Okay, so you stumbled. Welcome to the human race. If you're a fallible human being and not a god, you will diet imperfectly. Anything requiring discipline and dedication will probably not be perfectly followed by mortal human beings. Jumping into all-or-nothing thinking and grossly exaggerating a single mistake is clearly irrational. Your day journal will help you combat this kind of overblown self-recrimination. When you slip, you simply record your slip as one failure. Your ledger of success versus failure would look like this on the eleventh night of your diet: 32 meals on my diet, 1 meal off my diet. Current score: 32 to 1. Do you see how useful numbers can be in putting yourself back in contact with reality?

Yes, it's best to mightily resist even one slip; but if you do mess up, don't dump on yourself. Dummibrain will surely pull your depression lever. Then, once you're depressed, you'll probably feel like eating even more. Food, after all, is a notorious mood elevator. By all means, be critical of your behaviour, but not of yourself. Remember: you are not equivalent to one mistake.

What is serious about a mistake is not the fact that you acted imperfectly, the real concern is that one slip makes it easier to slip again. People who quit smoking know how true this is. A single cigarette makes it easier to smoke a second, then a third, until addiction once again rears its ugly head. The same holds true for a dieter who has just one little piece of cake or just one teeny piece of chocolate. As you know, one scoop of ice cream somehow makes the second scoop easier to eat.

So avoid fraudulent reasoning such as *What the hell, it's only one little cigarette. What harm can a few drags do?* And steer clear of self-deceptive promises such as *I'll enjoy this chocolate today, but I'll starve myself tomorrow.* We know that every slip paves the way for future slips. Practising slips makes you better at slipping. Keep the phony rationalizations out of your self-talk.

Work hard to avoid even a single slip, but when you slip (and you most certainly will), deal with it without laying your ego on the line. Don't rate your entire self as a failure because of one behavioural failure. A given **behaviour** can fail, but **you** cannot.

Okay, dear reader, this is one of those solemn moments when I feel constrained to enunciate one of my stunning eternal verities. I urge you to clasp this to your bosom and imprint it forever in your memory cells. *Never forget that you, as a human being, cannot be a failure. Only your acts can fail. You will fail only when you die.* If you absorb this single truth, you will have got

When you botch something only that single behaviour has failed.
You, as a human being cannot fail until you die.

your money's worth from this book. If the idea seems peculiar to you, keep thinking about it. Don't dismiss the notion out of hand. If you think about it long enough, it will sink in. And when it does, you will feel as though a great weight has been lifted from your life.

The knowledge that you cannot be a failure is a profoundly liberating revelation. Once you grasp this, you will free yourself to try countless new ventures. If you are like most human beings, you have shied away from many useful experiences because you felt you wouldn't do well. How ironic, how sadly ironic. We avoid doing what will give us growth because we're afraid we'll lose stature. We stunt our

> **The knowledge that you cannot be a failure is a profoundly liberating revelation.**

growth because we fear being magically diminished. If you're a victim of this malaise, I commend to you the words of the English essayist Gilbert Chesterton:

'Anything worth doing is worth doing poorly.'

Making mistakes won't turn you into an incredible shrinking man or woman.

7

I-Talk

There is a large body of verbal flimflam that obscures our true thoughts. Some of this gimmickry is conscious, some of it unconscious. Our use of linguistic trickery comes from many sources: simple habit, poor logic, shame, ignorance, exaggeration, issues of self-worth, the Jehovah complex, and so forth. Thus far, I have focused on **why** we play this verbal shell game. Now I want to look more closely at **how** the game is played. What are its rules? What are its signposts? Above all, how do we decipher it?

Much verbal hanky-panky comes in the guise of *I-talk*. I've already mentioned *I-can'tism*; so let me pick up where I left off. *I can't do X* literally means it's not possible for me to do X. If you ask me to leap over tall buildings in a single bound — I can't. If you ask me to outrace a speeding bullet — I can't. If you ask me to be more powerful than a locomotive — I can't.

In this sense, the *I can't* is clear and straightforward. In actual practice, however, it almost always has a veiled meaning. When you say, 'I can't', you rarely mean, *It's not humanly possible for me to do X*. In other words, you're using coded language.

The *I*, in expressions such as *I can't*, often is a signpost pointing toward hidden self-talk; so learn to heed this little duo of *I* plus *can't* whenever it pops up in your thoughts, and be prepared to do some translating. Fortunately, this decoding is usually easy. Let's suppose you and I are standing on a 30-foot diving platform. You urge me to jump. I take one look at the water and say 'No way. I can't do it.'

If my knees are knocking and my eyes are as big as saucers, you might reasonably conclude *I can't* really means *I'm scared*. As you probably already know, *I'm scared* is a common meaning for *I can't*. When my friend Fearful Fran is asked to speak before the PTA, she says, 'I'm sorry, I just can't speak before a group.' That, of course, is nonsense. Fran is simply scared.

Consider the many times Fran has thought about asking her boss for a rise. She hasn't had a rise for three years and it's long overdue; nonetheless, she keeps telling herself 'I can't ask my boss now. I'd better wait until business is better.' More poppycock. The fact is that Fran shakes in her boots every time she thinks about asking for a rise. If we examine her self-talk carefully, we find the fake *I can't* scattered throughout her scripts.

You may say, 'So what? What's the big deal? Nobody likes to admit they're afraid.' True, but that really isn't the issue. The question is whether Fran's 'harmless' self-deception is truly harmless. The denial of fearful feelings tends to surreptitiously freeze one's ability to act — a paralysis that can seriously hamper self-growth. Yes, we are sometimes embarrassed by our nutty fears, but self-growth requires that we face the magic in our thinking. We can grow only if we root out and challenge the crazy beliefs that immobilize us.

I urge you to keep a close watch on the *I can'ts* that appear in your self-talk. When you spot one, ask yourself if it really means, *This is not humanly possible for me to do.*

> I urge you to keep a close watch on the I can'ts that appear in your self-talk.

If it doesn't, ask yourself if it's a smoke screen for *I'm scared.*

Of course, 'I'm scared' isn't the only meaning of 'I can't'. I often say 'I can't sing' when what I really mean is 'I carry a tune rather badly.' If Melvin Moocher asks you for a loan and you say, 'Sorry, Melvin, I just can't,' you're really saying you don't want to. Or you won't. These kinds of linguistic ploys are seldom harmful, but all verbal camouflage has to be looked at with a suspicious eye.

Suppose you were working on self-assertiveness, and you said untruthfully, 'Melvin, I'd like to, but I just can't because I'm flat broke.' Would that help you reach your goal of being self-assertive? Or if I say I can't sing because I'm tone deaf, does that help me face my real fear, which is fear I'll be laughed at if I sing?

Verbal camouflage can hide some real anxiety — a fear generated by scary self-talk. If you're using a scary script, you had best find it, confront it, and work on replacing it with rational thinking. Never forget that Dummibrain is always listening, and you would be hard-pressed to overestimate his naïveté concerning words. If your I-talk can lead your thinking brain astray, imagine what it can do to your emotion-brain.

Another example of screwy I-talk can be seen in the title for Chapter 3, *I Never Do Anything Right*. This sentence begs to be translated. For starters, what would you use as a replacement for *I never*? Bear in mind that this exaggeration is almost always false and is usually hurtful. You can just as easily say such things as: *I rarely do X. I didn't succeed this time. I made a mistake. Sometimes I don't succeed. I haven't succeeded so far.*

Bear in mind that *I never* is a two-sided coin. The other side of the coin is *I always,* as in*: I always screw up. I always forget my grocery list. I always forget to close the windows. I always forget Emma's birthday.* Do you have any loony statements like these that you use in your self-talk? Try to recall some of them and record them in your day journal. Then think up some rational replacements. For starters, try *sometimes*, as in *Sometimes I forget my grocery list.*

In Chapter 4 we looked at the meaning of 'I must'. Be persistent in replacing this anti-scientific phrase. If you're talking about something you want to do, then say so. Simply say *I want to do X*. Why on earth should you pressure yourself to do what you want to do? If you're not enthusiastic about doing something, then say, *It would be in my best interest to do X.* Or try something like, *It would be preferable to do X. It would help me get what I want.* I used to have a poster in my office that said, *Musturbation is self-abuse.* Remind yourself of this when you detect another 'I must' in your self-talk.

Another damaging form of I-talk is the common phrase *I feel.* This often means, *I believe, I think.* I'm sure that saying *I feel* such and such seems rather harmless to most people; nonetheless, this guileless pair of words can cause considerable confusion in your thinking. Remember that one of the tasks you'll be facing in self-counselling is sorting out your thoughts and feelings. You will especially want to sharply delineate your irrational beliefs, but you'll be handicapped in digging out nutty ideas if you're confused about what a belief is.

> Another damaging form of I-talk is the common phrase I feel.

Think of a belief as something that is either true or false. You can gather evidence for or against a belief. In other words, you can challenge a belief. A feeling, on the other hand, is neither true nor false. You cannot gather evidence for or against a feeling. You cannot challenge a feeling. No evidence in the universe counts for or against a feeling. Feelings have nothing to do with truth or falsehood.

I realize I'm hammering this point, but this is a critical difference. You see, many people conveniently switch from *I believe* to *I feel* when they're clinging to an unsupportable belief. Does the following experience ring a bell for you? You are arguing an issue with a friend. To support your position, you marshal forth strong evidence backing your belief. You also point to some data that counts strongly against your friend's position. Your friend, in contrast, can produce no evidential basis for his screwy belief.

So what does your friend do? He says, 'Well, I don't care. I just **feel** it's true.' Presto! Your friend's belief has instantly become invulnerable to attack. Having been magically changed into a feeling, his belief is now sacrosanct. It has become impervious to rational questioning. This is on the same level as the statement, *I have a toothache.* It's what the philosophers call a *private datum.* How would you challenge such a claim? Has this happened to you in an argument? Were you annoyed? Of course you were. This subterfuge is an exasperating cop-out.

So what does this have to do with self-counselling? Simply this: sometimes people use this verbal chicanery to protect their nuttiest ideas from rational examination. So be suspicious of every *I feel* in your self-talk. Consider the case of Anxious Annie. She often protects her dotty ideas with I *feel* so and so. She's afraid to drive across bridges; so she says, 'I *feel* as though I'm going to somehow fall off the bridge.' She also has a problem with lifts. She won't ride in them because she 'feels' as though she's going to suffocate. Annie never says *I believe I'm going to fall off this bridge*, or *I believe I'm going to suffocate in this lift.* That sounds too crazy even for Annie; so she cops out and camouflages her nonsense with *I feel.*

Ironically, if we listen carefully, we can hear a tacit admission by Annie that her belief is not supported by evidence. She says things such as 'I don't know why, but I just feel that it's so.' Don't tolerate this waffling and wiggling in your self-talk. If you don't know why you believe something, you had best re-examine your belief — especially if it seems to be riling your emotion-brain.

I suggest you immediately translate *I-feel* sentences into *I-believe* sentences, unless you're referring to bodily sensations. If you're disguising a batty idea, get it out in the open. Force it to stand naked and lonely. Maybe then you'll be motivated to either support it or replace it.

Don't be afraid of uncovering nutty ideas in your thinking. You have a right to nutty ideas. My guess is that 100% of the human population holds irrational beliefs at one time or another. We are all fallible human beings, and we often use verbal camouflage to hide our often fallible thinking.

Amid the many I-talk cover-ups and follies, perhaps the most damaging is *I can't stand it.* This screwy thought usually occurs in conjunction with horribilizing. When judging a negative event, one thinks, *This is simply too awful for words. I can't stand it.*

If you spot this culprit in your self-talk, pounce on it with a vengeance. *I-can't-stand-it-itis,* as Dr Albert Ellis calls it, is an emotional crippler. Immediately challenge it with these thoughts: *This is obviously untrue. I **am** standing it at this very moment. That's absolute proof I can stand it. Okay, I admit I'm wailing and gnashing my teeth and tearing my hair. So what. That just proves I'm not standing it very well. Frankly, I would prefer to stand it better; nonetheless, I **am** standing it.*

Use your day journal to write some better coping scripts. Use sentences such as: *I certainly dislike X, and X has made me uncomfortable. I definitely don't like being uncomfortable, but it won't kill me. Instead of idiotically thinking I can't stand X, I think I'll focus on learning how to cope better. Whining is a waste of energy that doesn't change reality. Since I can't change X, I'll simply focus on coping better with X.*

When you say *I can't stand it*, you seriously risk stirring up an emotional upheaval. Think for a moment about how this sounds to Dummibrain. To him it sounds as though your survival is at stake, that the discomfort of X will crush you, that if X continues you'll surely die. Your emotion-brain responds by flooding you with fight-or-flight chemicals. The discomfort produced by these chemicals is then added to the discomfort you already have. Lucky you — you get two for the price of one. A bargain, I suspect, you did not wish for.

Dummibrain may fill you will immobilizing lethargy if you use the kind of I-talk we looked at in Chapter 2. *I am bad; I am worthless; I am a failure; I am incompetent; I am hopeless.* In this kind of I-talk, we recognize our old friend, the 'is' of identity. The easiest way to handle this insidious pest is to drastically reduce your use of the word am. To be constantly monitoring the use of 'am' would be a tedious task. Considering that almost every use of the word entails a global statement about the self, why not just avoid it whenever possible?

Bear in mind that I'm talking mostly about language likely to confuse Dummibrain. Obviously, if you say something, like *I'm a New Yorker*, you're not likely to create any problems. But the word 'am' is inherently loaded with exaggeration and usually is best avoided when working on your new self-talk.

Another suspicious form of I-talk is the *I don't* duo. This close relative of *I can't* often signals flim-flam. Consider Fearful Fran. While at a party she met a man she liked. She wanted to ask him to dance, but her debilitative *I-don'tism* interfered. She thought, *I can't ask him because **I don't** know him well enough. **I don't** dance well enough to get on the dance floor. **I don't** really feel like dancing at the moment. **I don't** know if I could handle it if he said no.* And so forth. Her dishonesty is transparent. She certainly *can* ask him to dance, and she can at least dance well enough to get on the dance floor. When you hear an 'I don't' in your self-talk, make sure it's honest.

To help you sort out your I-talk, I've assembled a table of common I-talk mistakes and some possible challenges. Make a table of your own or copy this one and put it on recipe cards. As you go about doing your linguistic housecleaning, keep referring to your I-talk cards. And while you're at it, make sure you aren't using any irrational I-talk in your day journal. Since your journal will be in the first person, you may easily slide into using dysfunctional I-statements.

I-talk	Challenges
I can't…	I'm scared. I don't want to. I won't. I don't do X very well.
I never…	I rarely. I didn't succeed this time. As a fallible being, I don't always succeed. Thus far, I haven't succeeded in doing X.
I'm a jerk	My behaviour was jerky, but that doesn't make me a jerk in my totality. I am fallible, and I will often make mistakes.
I must…	I want to. It would be in my best interest. I choose to do so, even though I don't have to.
I'm a failure.	I have not failed if I am alive. I only fail as a being when I die.

I-talk	Challenges
I am worthless.	Self-worth is a myth. Therefore, it is a useless concept. I can only rate my behaviour.
I am stupid because…	I did something dumb. That doesn't make my total self dumb.
I don't understand.	I don't like what I'm hearing. I refuse to accept it. Actually, I do understand.
I don't…	Am I being honest with myself when I say this? Am I failing to be assertive?
I always…	Sometimes I do X, I often do X. I'll work at doing X less often.
I can't stand it.	I am standing it at this very moment. I am stressing myself. I'm going to work at standing it better.
I shouldn't have…	I should have done X. All the prerequisites were in place. It seemed like a good idea at the time.
I feel that…	I believe X. I think that X is so. A belief can be true or false. A feeling is a bodily sensation.

I versus i, i, i, i, i, i, i, i, i, i, i, i, i…

You will note that I've included the phrase *I don't understand* in this table. This is another in the litany of the subterfuges we use to duck responsibility for our real thoughts. Take the case of Arnie. His sister Clara got mad and threw a frying pan at him. She just missed bouncing it off his head as he ducked out the kitchen door. Arnie angrily described the incident to me. As he talked, he kept punctuating his story with, 'I just don't understand how she could have done such a thing. She could have hurt me seriously; and after all I've done for her. What ingratitude.'

I wanted to challenge Arnie's use of 'I don't understand', but this is a ticklish undertaking. I tried using a little humour. I explained how Clara had curled her fingers around the handle of the frying pan, how she had lifted it over her head, how she had contracted her muscles, how she had propelled the pan through the air, and so forth. Arnie didn't appreciate this at all. He said, 'I don't understand how you can joke about something like this.' There it was again. I was faced with another *I don't understand*.

I wasn't merely joking. I was trying to get across a point. You see, Arnie undoubtedly *did* understand how Clara threw the frying pan. Understandably, he didn't like what she had done, and he considered her behaviour dangerous. But saying he does not understand merely cloaks Arnie's should-ing on reality.

I have often had difficult customers (DCs) in my support groups who doggedly and whiningly persist in saying, 'But I just don't understand.' What these DCs mean is that they don't like my analysis of a problem they're struggling with. This kind of stonewalling gets you nowhere. If you don't understand something, by all means, say so; however, if you do understand something, but you don't accept it, admit what you're doing — should-ing on others and the world. Then get on with the business of solving the problem as best as you can.

Far removed from the *I-don't-understand* mode is the *I-know-everything-in-your-mind* mode. This form of magical thinking has a covert linkage to where you locate yourself in the world. It ties in with a kind of grandiosity wherein you place yourself at the centre of everything happening in your environment. Most importantly, it connects with your placing yourself at the centre of what others are thinking and feeling. This attitude is, in other words, connected to plain old egocentrism.

Angry Arnie is good at this. He sees a woman laugh or smile, and he tells himself, *She's laughing at me. Who does she think she is? What a bitch.* Anxious Annie has a similar script. She sees somebody frown or grimace, and she tells herself, *He's angry at me. I'd better steer clear of him. He might hurt me. How awful.* Then there is Mournful Morrie. His daughter forgets to send him a birthday card, and he tells himself, 'She knows it's my birthday. She did this on purpose. She's deliberately trying to hurt me.'

The egocentric sees himself at the centre of the universe. Everything that happens within a certain radius seems directed at him. He suffers from negative grandiosity. He seems to think nobody has anything better to do than look for ways to put him down, make his life harder, or thwart his every desire.

This batty thinking is familiar to all counsellors. They even have a name for the method used to combat it: they call it *decentring.* A therapist would caution Arnie not to place himself at the centre of everything. The goal would be to teach Arnie that not every action, or inaction, is directed toward making his life miserable.

If you are working on decentring yourself, one signpost to watch out for is *me-talk.* Beware of thoughts such as, *He's laughing* **at me**. *He did that* **to me** *to hurt me.* Often the *at me* and *to me* are implied, as in *He's trying to put me down. She wants to give me the shaft. Somebody put that nail in my driveway to give me a flat tyre. My neighbour is playing loud rock just to bug me.* The exact words are not important. The key word to zero in on is *me. Me* is a strong clue. It represents your ego. It is your total self placed at centre stage in an unfolding drama — a kind of soap opera in which the world carries on a vendetta against you.

Me-talk is often associated with mind reading. If you look across a room at two smiling people and think 'George and Mary are laughing at me', you are in the grip of superstition. You are foolishly claiming the power to read minds. This kind of nonsense is all too common, and it needs constant challenging. Be vigilant. When you catch yourself mind reading, tell yourself such things as: *There I go magicking again. Who do I think I am? I must think I'm a wizard who operates beyond the laws of reality. What proof do I have that George and Mary are laughing at me? What is the probability they're laughing at me? One chance in a hundred? One chance in a thousand? What chance is there they're focused on me? Won't they have better things to think about?*

Think in terms of probability. Don't fret about mere possibility. Adopt a *probabilistic* orientation, not a *possibilistic* orientation. Sure, it's *possible* somebody left a nail in

> **Think in terms of probability.**

your driveway to give you a flat tyre, but it's not *probable*. You can drive yourself bonkers if you buy into the endless negative possibilities of life.

Challenge every idea you have that's not supported by evidence. If the notion that somebody left a nail in your driveway has no evidential basis whatsoever, reject it as a mere vagary that somehow jumped up out of your stream of consciousness. After all, that happens to everybody. We all have whimsical, crazy thoughts pop into our minds from time to time. The thing to remember is that rational people process and quickly dismiss these odd thoughts.

This constant reality checking is hard work, but it can eventually evolve into a mental habit — a psychological trait that pays great dividends. Don't forget to ask yourself which is easier — to energetically monitor your self-talk or to wallow in anxiety and depression.

Will you have to monitor and correct all forms of I-talk and me-talk? Of course not. As a matter of fact, the absence of the first person pronoun could be a warning signal. Consider a situation wherein somebody is violating your rights. When that happens, people often use *you-language*. This reflects a kind of thinking that blames other people.

Take the case of Angry Arnie. He's a classic blamer. The secretary at Arnie's office is often slow in typing his reports. This happens partly because she gives priority to typing reports for John, who just happens to be handsome and single. Needless to say, Angry Arnie is not one of her favourites, and Arnie's reports get pushed to the back burner. This results in Arnie being chewed out for being late with his reports.

So what does Arnie do? Like most injustice collectors, Arnie broods and broods. Finally he explodes in anger at the secretary. He screams, ***You*** *never get my reports done on time. Everybody in this office gets their reports done before mine. How did an* *incompetent like* **you** *ever get hired in the first place?* **You** *continually show favouritism.* **You** *always fail to keep your promises.* **You** *are slow, inefficient, and disorganized.* **You** *better shape up, or* **you** *will pay dearly.*

You, you, you, and you. This certainly qualifies as you-language. It also is clearly aggressive. Arnie is labelling, condemning, and threatening. He is mostly putting down the secretary. The proliferation of *yous* in his tirade signal what Arnie's focus is. He's focusing on the villainous secretary — not on his problem.

So what's the solution? After all, Arnie's rights are being disregarded. First of all, Arnie would do better if he didn't behave so angrily. To avoid this, he would be wise to use more I-language and less you-language. Suppose he said to the secretary, *Louise,* **I've** *been getting a lot of heat from the boss lately for handing in late reports. It sure has been unpleasant. Every time* **I** *get chewed out,* **I** *go home feeling in the dumps.* **I** *really work hard at my reports, and* **I** *think they're pretty good. But the boss loses sight of how good they are when* **I** *turn them in late.* **I** *sure would like to find a way to get them typed more speedily. Do you have any suggestions on how this could be done?*

Do you see how pronouns can be signposts of differing focuses? There are seven *yous* in the first example and seven *Is* in the second example. This reflects an important difference: in the first speech, Arnie *expresses* or displays his anger; in the second, he *states* how he feels.

Expression of anger usually involves being punitive toward others. On the other hand, when you simply state you feel unhappy, it doesn't put other people down or punish them. Expressing your anger usually escalates your anger. In other words, you become angrier as you air your complaint. When you simply state that you feel bad, it allows you to stay calm. In fact, as you state your case, you actually tend to feel better. Expressing your anger, in contrast, often leaves you feeling guilty after your tantrum. When you clearly state how you feel, it gives you a sense of satisfaction for having asserted yourself.

Perhaps the most damaging, and potentially dangerous, result of expressing anger is the possibility of retaliation from the other person, who may defend his or her self-worth like a cornered rat. Revealing one's feelings, on the other hand, is far more likely to elicit empathy and cooperation. Remember: *you-language* attacks, while *I-language* asserts. The difference is critical.

I realize that revealing feelings is a no-no in our culture — especially among males. I grew up seeing the John Wayne screen persona as the model of a strong, actualized human being. He embodied the 'strong, silent' type. We always heard those two words in tandem. Strong *and* silent. Silence and strength.

Beneath this pairing is a lie: the superstition that I'm stronger and healthier if I conceal my feelings. Beneath such silence there usually lies a dark sanctum of anxiety — a fear that others will think I'm weak if I reveal my inner self, a fear that others will use such knowledge as a weapon against me, a fear that others will not like or respect the real me.

The John Wayne persona is a cultural myth. Behind the façade is a flesh-and-bone person who probably feels loneliness, despair, and even deep terror. A woman who falls in love with a John Wayne mannequin may recoil with shock when the hidden self emerges.

Are you ready now for more great words of wisdom? These words are so important, I feel constrained to frame them.

> **If you pretend to be different from what you are, you will never know what it is like to be loved for what you truly are.**

Every time you express an opinion that isn't yours, think about this towering truth. Every time you parade your successes, but hide your failures, think about this. Every time you recount your moments of courage, but hide your moments of fear, think about this.

Hiding every wart and wrinkle makes it impossible to have deep, meaningful relationships. How can you draw close to another person if you can't share your doubts, your darkest fears, your anguish, your shame, your ecstasies, your crazy dreams?

Have you ever noticed that the Western screen hero never seemed to have true friendships with the women in his life? As for his male friends, he only seemed to express his 'love' for a friend through vengeance after the friend is murdered. The lives of these bloodless archetypes always seemed to be profoundly barren.

If you want another kind of life, one rich with friendships and close camaraderie, start telling your friends and lovers what's inside you. Oh sure, this sometimes backfires. The world is full of should-ers, and some so-called friends may should on you when you expose yourself. But your good friends will draw close to you. And why not? You will begin to seem far more human and lovable.

A couple of warnings as you set about being more open with people. Above all, be prudent. It may not be a good idea to tell your boss about your foibles and self-doubts. Not everybody is an appropriate confidante. Second, don't go overboard and become a whiner. Don't start describing and lamenting your every woe to others. If you do, they'll start running fast when they see you coming.

As a final note, I leave you with a brief look at the consequences of stating your anger versus expressing your anger.

I-language versus You-language

When you say that you feel anger...	When you manifest your anger...
it doesn't put others down.	you are usually punishing somebody.
it tends to calm you.	it increases your anger.
it usually gives you feelings of satisfaction.	it often leaves you feeling guilty.
it wins more cooperation from others.	it sometimes triggers retaliation.

8

Death by Qualification and Other Follies

> 6 Complete rationality is no doubt an unattainable ideal, but so long as we continue to classify some men as lunatics it is clear that we think some men are more rational than others. I believe that all solid progress in the world consists of an increase in rationality, both practical and theoretical. 9
>
> Bertrand Russell

Have you ever thought about what constitutes an insane belief? It's easy to come up with examples, but how would you *define* a crazy belief? What are its defining characteristics? Doubtlessly the belief must be false. After all, we don't call a belief nutty if it's true. Suppose somebody believes X, and X is clearly false. Further suppose the believer is shown mountains of evidence, but he or she persists in believing X. Are we entitled to say that person is missing a few marbles? Perhaps. But let's take a closer look.

Suppose Loony Louie believes something we know to be false — he insists he is Napoleon Bonaparte. He wears funny hats, swaggers around with one hand tucked in his shirt, and keeps asking for Josephine. We try to reason with Louie. We show him history books, encyclopedias, historical diaries, and an eyewitness account of Napoleon's death in 1821. We invoke the sciences of biology and physics to prove Napoleon is dead.

But nothing dents Louie's belief regarding his identity. Finally, Louie's family takes him to Europe and shows him the corpse of Napoleon. All to no avail. Louie stubbornly assures us history has been grossly falsified, that science doesn't know everything about longevity, and that the corpse was surely that of someone else.

Despite massive evidence counting against his claim, Louie will not yield. As a last resort, we ask him to prove he is Napoleon. He tells us it's our job to disprove he is Napoleon. But how can we? Louie seems to ignore a basic rule of science. It's called the *verifiability principle*. This rule says a belief should be testable (at least in theory). Other people must be able to check it out. A neutral scientist should be able to prove Louie is really Napoleon by using the same method Louie uses, whatever that might be.

I've been urging you to respect the verifiability principle in your self-talk. The question *Where is my proof?* is one I urge you to ask about any upsetting thought you have. This question affirms the need to test the truth of your claims. Neurotics never seem to question the validity of their irrational beliefs. If somebody questions their beliefs, they simply discount all counterevidence.

This stonewalling against all logic and evidence had me puzzled for years. I struggled to find a way to deal with it. Then I came across a brief essay by the British philosopher Antony Flew. In his essay, Flew introduced his concept of *death by qualification*. I became excited when I realized that Flew was describing the same ploy used by countless neurotics — gimmicks that had frustrated me for years.

In order to teach the members of my support groups how this fallacy operates, I devised a teaching tool I labelled *the dragon game*. I played this game in college classes and in support groups. We played the game much like the following imaginary game.

Group facilitator: Richard Franklin.
Group members: Arnie, Irene, Fran, Annie, Morrie, Bill.

Franklin: *Okay, group, today I want to play a little game. It may seem silly to you, but bear with me. I have a serious purpose. Be patient, and do your best to contribute. Do what film buffs do: engage in a willing suspension of disbelief.*

I'm going to start the game by saying something rather odd. Nonetheless, I want everybody to treat it as a serious announcement. Okay?

While hiking in the woods one fine day, I came across a fire-breathing dragon. Naturally I was elated by my discovery. Trembling with excitement, I enticed the beast into following me home, where I locked it in my garage.

The basic belief you are now confronted with is this: I, Richard Franklin, have a fire-breathing dragon locked in my garage. Does anybody believe this? (No hands are raised.) *All right, unbelievers. I challenge you to find a way to test my belief and prove I'm wrong. Irene, what would you do to refute my claim?*

Irene: *I'd start with something simple. I'd visit your garage and look in the window. Following that, I'd report I had seen nothing.*

Franklin: *I agree. That would be the easiest approach. I forgot, however, to mention that this dragon has the power to make himself invisible. Any other suggestions?*

Bill: *I'd sprinkle flour on the garage floor and watch for footprints.*

Franklin: *A clever idea, Bill. One problem though: this dragon is weightless.* (Groans from the group.)

Annie: *We could put a fast-reacting thermometer in the room and watch for sudden rises in heat. That would tell us whether the dragon was really spitting fire.*

Franklin: *An excellent idea; however, I forgot to tell you this dragon generates heatless fire.*

Arnie: *I'd get a paint sprayer and spray the dragon with paint so we could see him.*

Franklin: *Good thinking. The only trouble is my dragon can make himself incorporeal, in which case the paint would merely drift through him.*

Frank:	*I'd go over to the physics departments of the university and borrow a hydrogen sulphide gas detector, which could be used to record gas emissions from the dragon.*
Franklin:	*A very scientific approach; however, this dragon is odourless and gasless.* (More groans from the group.)
Morrie:	*Okay, I say we run a gravitational test. The dragon must have some mass if he exists. We could hang a steel ball on a string and borrow instruments from the university to measure the force of the pull between the two masses — the mass of the dragon and the mass of the steel ball.*
Franklin:	*Aha! We have another physics student among us. I guess I should have been more precise when I said the dragon was weightless. What I meant was the dragon has no measurable mass.*
Frank:	*I'm having trouble understanding what it means when you say this dragon exists. For the sake of argument, I'll concede he has no measurable mass. But surely he must have some molecular structure. Why not pass microwaves through him and jiggle his water molecules? That would produce friction heat, which would make the dragon boil and steam.*
Franklin:	*That may well be true, but he would only produce invisible steam due to his unique molecular structure.*
Frank:	*But wouldn't he howl when he started to boil?*
Franklin:	*One would certainly think so, but this dragon howls at a frequency that is impossible to measure or detect.* (Hissing and booing from the group.)
Irene:	*I think we're entitled to say there is no such dragon. All our tests fail to show us anything. This is strong evidence for claiming there is no such animal in your garage. I maintain you don't have a shred of evidence to support your bizarre claim. All we have is your rather peculiar belief,*

and that hardly qualifies as evidence. The truth is, I can't even understand what you're saying.

*Please tell me, **what is the difference between your odourless, noiseless, weightless, heatless, gasless, invisible, bashful dragon and no dragon whatsoever?***

Franklin: *Wonderful. I applaud your fine insight. You have asked a great question. Since I've steadfastly qualified my belief so as to reject every test you can come up with, you are entitled to wonder what is the difference between my dragon and a non-dragon.*

Even so, there is an even more crucial question. It's the key question you must always ask of those who endlessly qualify fantastic claims. Think hard. What other question occurs to you?

Irene: *I was about to follow up with this question: **what conceivable evidence would count against your belief?** Surely you can think of something that would count against the truth of your claim. Can you give us a single example that would, in your wildest imagination, count against your belief? Can you tell us exactly what it is that you would accept as counterevidence?*

Franklin: *Beautiful. You have hit on **the** key question. That's the question you should always ask whenever somebody peddles any belief that seems to be impervious to all counterevidence. Never hesitate to ask this question when myth peddlers defend their nonsense by means of constant qualification.*

In answer to your question, I can't think of any evidence whatsoever that would count against my belief.

Morrie: *I'm wondering what difference it makes whether your belief is true or not. The world will remain exactly the same in either case. Using your system, a person would be entitled to believe any metaphysical twaddle whatsoever.*

Franklin: *Exactly.*

You may think this game is rather silly and little more than an ivory-tower diversion; nonetheless, I've had many chances to use the principles it illustrates. Take the case of Ellie, a member of a support group. She put herself on a faddish brown-rice diet. Over a period of a year, her skin became dry and scaly; her face became gaunt; her eyes lost their sparkle; her lips became cracked and shrivelled; and her hair began falling out.

It was hard to believe Ellie had once radiated good health and was bursting with physical energy. I was dismayed by the changes I saw. I tried to reason with her and convince her to take a hard look at her diet. All to no avail. Ellie followed her diet with religious zeal. I tried showing her scientific data to the effect that her diet might damage her nervous system. She rejected these studies out of hand. She claimed the studies were biased and unscientific. Any studies that ran counter to her dietary claims were labeled 'unscientific'.

One day I asked Ellie to tell me what evidence might conceivably count against her belief in a diet that was clearly sapping her health. I told her to use the farthest stretches of her imagination and to explore her wildest fantasies to come up with a single example of what would count against the scientific validity of her diet. She was unable to fantasize a single piece of evidence what would count against her beliefs concerning her Spartan diet.

Eventually, I made the same request as a homework assignment. I explained how her belief would be meaningless if nothing could conceivably ever count against it. Ellie finally agreed to accept the challenge. As she struggled to do her homework, Ellie finally saw how irrationally she had been clinging to her belief.

Next, I asked her to do some minor tinkering with her diet. She finally agreed it would be irrational to reject any experimenting whatsoever. She began adding a few new foods to her diet. Within a few months she began to gain weight, her hair stopped falling out, and her skin began to recover its former glow.

Have you ever believed something with Ellie's stubbornness? Have you ever hedged a dearly held belief with endless qualifications? Think about what you do when new information challenges your most cherished beliefs. Are you guarding a dragon in your garage?

Now let's return to the dragon game and my imaginary support group.

Franklin:	*Can you see how this concept applies to Self-Counselling?*
Irene:	*Could you give us an example?*
Franklin:	*Okay, suppose that one day I come to our weekly meeting feeling depressed. I tell the group I'm a total failure, and that I haven't accomplished one worthwhile thing in my life. How would you challenge this?*
Bill:	*I'd point out that you have an advanced degree.*
Franklin:	*Yes but any fool can get a degree nowadays. You can even buy them through the mail. I've met all sorts of fools with degrees. It doesn't mean a thing.*
Fran:	*But you've written and published several books.*
Franklin:	*For some reason, that seems to impress people. Look at the trash that's printed nowadays. People are superstitiously reverent about the printed word. Getting a little ink means nothing. I may fool a few people, but I know the stuff I've published is junk.*
Arnie:	*You have a good reputation as a teacher.*
Franklin:	*That doesn't mean I've done anything new or valuable in my field. It only means a few gullible people think so.*
Irene:	*You make a good living.*
Franklin:	*So what? I could make more money selling dope on the street corners of Los Angeles.*
Annie:	*Okay, I'll be the one to bite and ask the grand question. Just what will you accept as evidence against your belief you are a professional failure?*
Franklin:	*Well, since I'm the only one who knows what a phony I am, I can't accept anything as counterevidence.*
Bill:	*In others words, what you say is **immune to evidence**?*
Franklin:	*Exactly.*

What I'm trying to underscore with this game is an important principle of sane thinking — *the principle of holding a belief tentatively.* That is to say, if new information comes along that counts against your belief, you had better re-examine that belief. If somebody sails around the world, it's time to stop believing the world is flat. When you read the health data for smokers, you'd better stop believing cigarettes can't harm you. When I show you how your procrastination is an emotional problem, you had better open your mind to that possibility.

Be prepared to question your beliefs. Don't put on blinkers once you've embraced an appealing belief. *The truth of a belief is more important than how attractive that belief is.* Listen to new information. Look at new ways of seeing a problem. Many of the claims I present in this book are angrily rejected by people the first time they hear them but they eventually accept them.

> **Be prepared to question your beliefs.**

A woman came to my therapy group for the first time on a night when we were discussing the myth of self-worth. As soon as she heard me refer to self-worth as a myth, she stormed out of the meeting. She had no wish to hear any more. I've seen mental health professionals walk out of lectures by Dr Albert Ellis. They were unwilling to stay and hear his reasoning or his clinical evidence.

Always keep in mind that you cannot be diminished by a questioning of your beliefs. On the contrary, having a questioning attitude can help you grow. Don't invest your 'self-worth' in your beliefs. If your belief is mistaken, *you* do not magically become a mistake. The great philosopher Bertrand Russell spent years developing a philosophical theory. Then his theory came tumbling down when one of his own students, Ludwig Wittgenstein, pointed out some serious flaws. Russell was stunned; nonetheless, he quickly recovered and became highly excited over Wittgenstein's contribution. Russell instinctively focused on **what** he was doing, not on **how well** he was doing. You could do worse than follow Russell's example.

Bertrand Russell, who had one of the greatest minds of the twentieth century, was always willing and eager to listen. Many of us find it hard to have this openness about dearly held beliefs. We take certain beliefs and lock them behind fences. We seal them off and jealously protect them from any threats. Russell believed that most people have 'pockets of insanity', especially in politics and religion.

Over a century ago, the psychologist Bernard Hart labelled these pockets *logic-tight compartments.* Hart argued that these intellectual bunkers are the essence of what society labels as 'insanity'. He was one of the first to note how society gives its stamp of approval to such cubicles when established in areas such as religion and politics. He then mused over the fact that society calls it *'insanity'* when people establish the same logic-tight compartments in other areas. Beliefs about identity, for example, must be rational. If you believe you are Napoleon, and you refuse to accept evidence to the contrary, you may end up in an asylum.

Defined this way, *insanity* is relative. Do you have any logic-tight compartments? I'll bet you do. If so, I urge you to open the hatches and air out these intellectually fetid holes with the fresh air of honest questioning.

Logic-tight compartments are only one form of fallacy. I've touched on others throughout this book: circular reasoning, all-or-nothing thinking, and so forth. Since we sometimes use these fallacies to disguise screwy self-talk, let's give some of them a closer look.

All-or-nothing thinking

All-or-nothing may be the most damaging of the common fallacies. It's often allied with perfectionism. If you can't do a task 100% perfectly, you have totally failed. If you got an A in history, but your friend Susan gets an A+, you've failed the course. If you don't beat Jack at golf, a gorgeous summer day is completely ruined. If your lover isn't 100% loving and sexual 100% of the time, he or she doesn't love you anymore. If the system of justice doesn't work perfectly, it is totally and universally unfair.

If you make one mistake, it's one of those days when absolutely nothing goes right.

This fallacy is a deadly one. Work hard at purging it from your self-talk. Seeing everything in black or white can slowly squeeze the joy out of life. This bipolar vision can block you from trying new things, make you demanding in your personal relationships, and seal you off from much that is beautiful in life. Keep reminding yourself that few things are entirely good or bad. Your performance, your lover's behaviour, your frustrations at work, and countless other spheres of your life fall into grey areas. The real world is coloured in endless shades of grey.

Bipolarism in your thinking will forever have you sitting at one end zone or another; however, the best seats in the stadium aren't located at the two end zones — they're at the 50-yard line. This is where you want to place yourself in the game of life. In particular, this is where you want to anchor your performance. By that I mean a normal achievement would be situated at the middle of the playing field. When you do well, you can rate your performance at 60. If you do fantastically, you can give it a rating of 75. If you do poorly, rate your endeavor at 40. If you do abysmally, assign a score of 25. My point is that it's best to tie all ratings to the 50-yard marker. Never assign scores of less than 15 or more than 85. A score of 85, after all, is an increase of 35 over what you normally do.

I'm asking you to base your thinking on reality. By putting your normal performance at 50, you are not giving it a score of 50; you are using this as a point of reference. This will give you a rational perspective for judging your relative successes and failures. By seating yourself at the 50-yard line, you will put maximum distance between yourself and the deadly absolutes of zero and 100.

False dilemma

False dilemma is the first cousin of the all-or-nothing fallacy. We all face true dilemmas in our lives. Choices are frequently tough.

Should I get a divorce and leave my kids with one custodial parent? Should I quit this secure-but-dead-end job and start looking for something else? Should I move to a drier climate to help my asthma and leave all my friends? Should I have back surgery or not?

Back surgery is something I've been thinking about for a long time. If I don't have surgery, I may spend the rest of my life with chronic pain. If I do go under the knife, I could quite possibly end up worse than I am now. I can, of course, look for a third choice. If I find a third path that is more palatable, I will be going through the horns of the dilemma. If I choose surgery, I will be taking the dilemma by one horn.

False dilemmas are two in kind:

1. You horribilize over your two choices, when one of the choices is merely uncomfortable. You tell yourself something like, *These are horrible choices. I know I couldn't stand either one. How unfair! Why should I have to choose between such dreadful options?*
2. You blind yourself to other possibilities. You are so focused on the 'horror' of your dilemma that you don't see an obvious third choice. You create a morbid tunnel vision with your horribilizing.

Mournful Morrie is into the first type of false dilemma. Morrie hasn't been getting along with his lover, Cathy. They've been squabbling for months, and they can't seem to get back on track. Morrie deeply enjoys Cathy's companionship, her affection, and her sexuality. But he hates their frequent quarrels, which leave him deeply depressed. Morrie thinks he'll go on forever in a strife-ridden relationship or break up with Cathy and spend the rest of his life as a lonely bachelor.

The second of these choices is highly unlikely. Morrie is a handsome young man with a good job, who would most likely find another partner. And even if he didn't, it would not be flat out 'horrible' as Morrie supposes. The fact is that one horn of the dilemma is simply not as ghastly as Morrie irrationally thinks.

But let's suppose, for the sake of discussion, Morrie actually does face two 'horrible' choices. The fallacy here is in thinking that only two choices exist. Often there is an option that takes us between the horns of an alleged dilemma. Morrie unfortunately has blinded himself to other options. Since he and Cathy are basically compatible, they stand a chance of working out their minor frictions through rational joint counselling.

It would help, of course, if Morrie were to rewrite his whining script. He would do well to seek out and challenge (1) any horribilizing, (2) any I-can't-stand-it-itis, and (3) any Jehovian demands that things be different from what they are. He could then focus on his problem — an admittedly knotty situation, but one that is in no way extraordinary or unsolvable.

Now we come to a form of sorcery I have already touched on in Chapter 2 while discussing the myth of self-worth.

Word superstition

Semantic voodoo comes in many forms, but I want to discuss a particular form of word magic. Logicians call it reification. You reify when you believe a word *must* correspond to something in objective reality. Reifiers superstitiously see a word that seems to name something as evidence that such a thing exists. Children do this glibly. Since we have words such as *ghosts*, *goblins*, and *witches*, a child tends to think these words must refer to something in the world.

Unfortunately, adults reify with equal abandon. The only difference is that adults do it with more abstract words. They don't actually have any idea of what these words refer to, but they are convinced they refer to some **thing** in the world.

Consider the abstract word 'destiny'. During its expansionary years, America came to believe in a doctrine called *manifest destiny*. America was **destined** to stretch across the continent. Passionate speeches thundered in the halls of Congress. Pulpit, press, and podium shook with feisty oratory about America's inevitable role in history. American leaders seemed to be describing some higher force that was shaping American history and adding huge chunks of territory to the American domain. What this force was, nobody really knew, a something that probably was no more than greed. Manifest destiny was, and is, pure twaddle.

Many individuals use similar words when talking about their lives. Words such as *fate*, *karma*, *kismet*, and *luck* abound in the vocabulary of many, people who ironically often lead direction-less lives. They believe there is some force intervening in their lives — usually to jinx them or bless them. Many neurotics, for example, see their lives as being constantly jinxed by bad luck.

This belief reinforces their grim views of the future. I've coun-selled these doomsayers in support groups. If I suggest to them that they follow specific courses of action, they come up with answers such as, *Oh, I can't do that. That's just not me. That's not my karma.* With that kind of attitude, a person may stay for years in an unhappy marriage, stay with a hateful job, or go on raising kids in a dangerous neighbourhood. If you tell such a person he's being superstitious, he acts amazed. Yet that is pre-cisely what is going on. He reifies words such as *luck* or *fate* to explain his predicament. This is no different from thinking a crop failure is caused by the wrath of an angry god.

Do you believe in luck? If so, you are in the grip of a blatant superstition. You believe, in effect, that some force or god is intervening in human affairs so as to favour or jinx targeted sub-jects. There is no evidence for the existence of a force such as luck. There are only probabilities. Fortunately, we can often work to change those probabilities. The lifestyle you adopt will directly affect the specific probabilities in your life. If you become a bank robber, for example, you increase the probability that you will end up in prison. And so on.

Attitude also affects probabilities. Take Fearful Fran. She has a powerful fear of failure. As a result, when a good opportunity comes along, Fran stalls and what-ifs endlessly. Finally, the chance passes her by.

Fran is often envious of her friend Rachel. She thinks Rachel is one of the luckiest people in the world. Rachel earns the same modest salary as Fran; nonetheless, in ten years Rachel has bought six duplexes and four single houses. Every year her cash flow is improving. She plans to acquire a few more properties and eventually retire at an early age.

Fran would often whine about Rachel's fantastic 'luck' in finding good deals in real estate. Finally, Rachel felt sorry for Fran; so one day she took Fran to see a terrific buy on a small house. The owner was willing to sell with nothing down. Best of all, as a rental property it would have a small cash flow. Fran isn't stupid, and she saw immediately that it was a good deal.

Alas, that's when the what-iffing started. Fran developed headaches, insomnia and heartburn. She stalled and stalled. Eventually, another buyer snapped up the property. Rachel, of course, no longer shows these good deals to Fran. And Fran? She's still sitting around whining about her 'bad luck'.

Next, we have the case of Irene. Irene says she's 'unlucky at love.' She thinks her pal Sally, on the other hand, is truly blessed in finding love. When Irene and Sally go to a party together, Sally always seems to meet a really nice guy, while Irene seems to meet nothing but 'jerks'.

A close look at Irene's attitudes tells us why she only meets 'jerks'. Irene is a feminist. Fine, so is her friend Sally. The difference is that Irene is exceptionally militant and angry in her brand of feminism. The fact is she carries a big chip on her shoulder. When she meets a man, she automatically puts the conversation on an adversarial plane. It becomes a form of competition. She is determined to prove she's no 'bubblehead' and is as smart or smarter than any man.

As a result, a man cannot express an opinion without having Irene attack what he is saying. If the guy says it looks like rain, Irene immediately points out that the clouds 'obviously' are not rain clouds. If he says he likes the essays of Gore Vidal, she immediately compares them to the work of Joan Didion, her favorite essayist, and labels Vidal 'superficial' by comparison. If the guy says he likes country western music, she argues that such music is shallow and sexist. Only jazz is worth listening to. And so forth.

The war of the sexes is on. Irene's conversations with men are combat zones. The result is predictable — men rarely ask her out. Sally, in contrast, is often asked out. Yes, Sally is the lucky one. The men she meets are nice guys. They aren't hostile and argumentative like the men Irene meets. Poor Irene. She sure has rotten luck.

The lesson is clear. Purge the word *luck* from your vocabulary. Also remove words such as *destiny, fate, karma.* A rational person looks at probabilities. He or she asks, *How can I increase the probabilities of getting what I want?* Fran could increase the probabilities of getting financial rewards by overcoming her fear of failure. Irene could increase the probability of finding a man by changing her bellicose conversational style. In both cases, they had best expunge the word-magic from their thinking and face the fact that there is no such thing as luck.

The reification of *luck* is only one example among thousands. One example I often refer to is the use of the words *thought* and *emotion.* Simply because we have these two distinct words, almost everybody automatically believes there must be two distinct things to which these two words refer. They ask themselves, *Why else would we have two words?* They assume there must be two entities floating around in the world that correspond to these words.

This assumption is poppycock. Our vocabularies are groaning under the weight of thousands of words that refer to absolutely nothing in objective reality. As you gain more skill in your rational self-counselling, you will notice that when you replace an angry thought with a non-angry thought, your anger disappears. You see, for all practical purposes, your angry thought *is* your anger. Think about it. When you replace an angry script, your anger leaves you. This suggests that emotions are basically clusters of self-talk.

So why do we need two terms such as *thought* and *emotion*? They seem to refer to a single event — a particular self-talk script. There is a script for anger, one for anxiety, one for depression, one for calm, one for simple irritation, and so forth. There is an old principle in philosophy called *Occam's razor.* This rule says we are better served if we don't create more things than necessary to explain something. If we have several explanations for some phenomenon, we are usually better served if we pick the simplest theory.

Consider the case of Fran's failure in real estate. If we have a perfectly good explanation that can be verified experimentally, why should we add another factor such as luck? After all, we can't even begin to refute or verify such abstract nonsense as luck or karma.

You may want to quarrel with my definition of emotion because you confuse bodily sensations and emotions. It's true you will have strong bodily feelings in tandem with emotions such as anger or fear. But these are simply bodily concomitants triggered by the old brain. Bear in mind that you will always have some bodily sensations and that you are therefore always in some feeling state — be it serenity or turmoil. Any thought-emotion has an effect on your body. This is simply a physical feedback.

Remember that your old brain prepares your body for given situations. If you are using fearful self-talk, your body will start pumping adrenaline. Your muscles will tense, and your pupils will dilate. This prepares you for fight or flight. But is this all we mean when we speak of emotion? I hardly think so.

> Remember that your old brain prepares your body for given situations.

Think of what you are feeling in your body as a symptom of your emotion -— not the emotion itself. After all, nobody confuses jaundice and hepatitis. Turning yellow is a symptom of hepatitis — it is not the disease itself. Or take a simple headache. You wouldn't confuse it with the anger you're feeling toward your boss.

You will find that, for all practical purposes, your self-talk scripts *are* your emotions. I realize you may feel uneasy with this radically new definition. If that is the case, use this definition simply because it's useful. Take the practical advice of William of Occam and prune unnecessary entities from your world view. Use what works. The fact is that most mental health professionals have no idea what emotions are or where they come from. So why not adopt the clear and practical definition I offer you? Let others wallow in their psychobabble while you get on with the business of living.

⬤ Bandwagon thinking

At the time I wrote this book I was living in Southern California, where there always seem to be some new or frenzied fads in such things as food, pop psychology and assorted forms of mystical voodoo. These movements seem to spring up overnight and ride on a crest of exaggerated claims as their spokespersons swindle people out of their money, physical health and emotional stability. Each new craze has its nabobs and gurus, its mystics and seers, its prophets and messiahs.

The enthusiasm of these often magnetic preachers can be admittedly attractive. For many, it feels exciting to hop on one of these bandwagons. The variety is endless. Colonic irrigation, walking on hot coals, astral projection, necromancy, reincarnation, astrology, fortune-telling, thought control, mind reading, séances, one-food diets, rebirthing, Rolfing, visualization, and so on.

Sometimes these manias begin with a seed of truth, but this is soon lost in a sea of absurd claims. Take visualization. It can be an excellent tool for self-counselling and personal growth. But some of its disciples make outlandish claims. An otherwise intelligent California schoolteacher once solemnly assured me that if she ever lost a limb, she could grow a new one with visualization.

It's hard to explain how intelligent people become so irrational. Bandwagon thinking seems to significantly undermine the ability to reason. Human beings have a propensity to succumb to the authority of numbers. But large numbers do not make a belief true. Hundreds of millions of people hold astoundingly irrational beliefs. Resist the weight of numbers. Don't buy into beliefs because they are the *in* thing.

Embracing baseless beliefs, even if believed by vast numbers of people, will rarely do you any good, and it may do you serious harm. Make it a mental habit to require concrete evidence before you accept a belief. Reject abstractions that can't be reduced to concrete particulars. Don't accept hearsay examples or anecdotal evidence. Last, but not least, heed this caveat: *Don't believe everything you read or hear in the media.*

A teacher of mine once told me, 'Throughout all recorded history, the majority has always been wrong.' I had to chew on that for a while. He was saying new truths are not discovered by masses of people. Most often it is a single individual who first perceives a new truth. Can you imagine being the only person in the world to hold a new belief? Imagine Anton van Leeuwenhoek's feelings when he peered through the world's first microscope and saw myriads of little bugs swimming about furiously in a drop of water. Imagine the derision he faced when he excitedly announced to the world, 'Our water is filled with little swimming bugs!'

Fortunately, science ultimately prevailed as the new world of microscopic organisms was revealed. Sadly, many of the so-called life sciences have not done so well. Bandwagon thinking has held back progress in psychology since its inception. Sigmund Freud spun a fanciful and elaborate theory to explain human emotions. Although there was little reason to believe Freud was right, his mystical determinism ruled triumphantly over psychotherapy for decades. The Freudian bandwagon became a juggernaut rolling over those who protested and asked for plausible evidence supporting Freud's armchair theories. His arcane doctrines, in one form or another, still permeate much thinking in psychology. The vocabulary changes, but the basic notions persist in many faddish self-help theories.

For years I've watched another bandwagon rolling. Let's call it the *disease bandwagon.* Its presence is especially noticeable in the treatment of alcoholism. Hospitals and clinics often offer treatment programmes that categorize chronically heavy drinkers as people afflicted with a *disease.* This alleged disease has powers not unlike my fire-breathing dragon. Even after an addict has been dried out and is no longer addicted, even after his body has returned to a normal homeostasis, even after his physiology no longer craves periodic doses of alcohol — he is still seen as *diseased.* And even though he never takes another drink, he carries this mysterious, invisible, incurable disease to the grave. It's time we recognized that the dominant thinking about alcoholism is so saturated with superstitions, word magic, contradiction, and cultism, it's a small miracle any alcoholics ever recover.

Disease is a useful metaphor, but a metaphor is not reality. If I say Henry is a bulldog, I am not saying he has a tail, walks on all fours and barks. I'm merely using a metaphor which suggests Henry is tenacious. I certainly am not suggesting Henry compulsively chases cats and almost certainly will do so for the rest of his life.

The irony of the disease metaphor is that it is never used to describe addiction to tobacco. Yet smokers are hooked on one of the most addictive substances known to science. Once a smoker stops smoking and his bodily addiction is gone, he is no longer called a smoker or tobacco addict. Nobody says he'll be suffering from *nicotinism* for the rest of his life. It would be considered rather odd to a call a nonsmoker a *nicotinolic.* Imagine this introduction being spoken by a former smoker: 'Good evening, folks. My name is Fred, and I'm a nicotinolic.'

Unfortunately, the *disease-disease* is spreading. It seems as though innumerable behaviours are being hoisted aboard the disease bandwagon. An array of clinics and costly programmes go so far as to say that we have a disease if we overeat. Then, they coyly tell us, we have a disease if we undereat. You have a disease if you gamble, shoplift, or overuse your credit cards. Many people still cling to the baseless belief that if you do naughty things with members of the same sex, you have a disease called homosexuality.

Perhaps we should enter the disease bandwagons in the St Patricks Day Parade. What a motley crew of patients it would display: fat people, skinny people, former boozers, spendthrifts, gamblers, gays, lesbians, and bisexuals. Skinny homosexual spendthrift ex-drinkers would be prominently displayed for having four diseases at once. This bandwagon would have a good chance of winning the parade's fantasy award.

Don't let bandwagon thinking affix labels to you. The *is* of identity is a powerful word in our self-talk. When you tell yourself 'I *am* a smoker,' you imply that smoking is your essence. Stick to labelling your behaviour. You will be better able to change your behaviour by focusing on it. Equating the self with a bad behaviour usually leads to guilt and self-condemnation. This, in turn, leads to more smoking, drinking, and overeating. I know these thoughts will risk the wrath of many in the medical and counselling community, but when you see little bugs in the water, you see little bugs in the water.

Mind reading

You will find mind reading described in many self-help books, and with good reason. It's a hurtful habit. People who would never claim the ability to walk on water or levitate or make themselves invisible or see through walls, nonetheless seem to believe they can read other people's minds. Angry Arnie, for example, insists he always knows what his sister is thinking. He tells me, 'I've been living with Clara too long not to know her every mood and thought. I can tell in an instant when she's mad or worried about something. And I always know when she's lying.' Does this sound familiar to you? Have you ever had similar thoughts about somebody you're close to?

Arnie, of course, is usually mistaken. And Clara, as we might expect, is unhappily frustrated by Arnie's ridiculous mind reading. She is often downright flabbergasted by many of Arnie's suspicions about her thoughts. Worse yet, she never seems to be able to dissuade Arnie once his mind is made up.

Arnie has even learned how to provoke Clara so that his belief is verified by her response. If he thinks Clara is angry, he nags and pesters her until she finally blows up. Then he triumphantly says, 'Aha! See, I told you so. I knew you were mad at me.' This technique, by the way, is often used in screwball encounter groups. Group leaders become skilled at instigating anger in otherwise non-angry people. They then use this provoked anger to 'prove' the client is not in touch with his or her feelings. I must admit, I find it easy to get angry at such manipulative hogwash.

If you use mind reading, and you probably do, you'll bungle it as badly as Arnie. We're all hopelessly inept at reading other minds. If you persist in trying, I predict you'll botch it nearly every time. Yes, I know it's a great temptation in love relationships. But bungled mind reading is second only to anger as a cause of marital and romantic breakups. There is so much wishful thinking and insecurity in many love relationships, any mind reading usually spells big trouble.

To counteract the common propensity to read minds, ask yourself, *Where's my proof?* If you think your sweetheart no longer loves you, ask yourself how you know this. If you think your boss is angry at you, make sure you have some concrete evidence to base your thought on. If you think your doctor is hiding the truth from you, ask yourself how probable it is. Don't be possibilistic; be probabilistic. How probable is it that your thought is true? Even more to the point, how probable is it you can successfully read minds?

Try the following exercise to help understand how mind reading works. Go to a suitable ethnic restaurant. Pick one where the patrons speak with animated use of the hands and greater volume than we use in English. Select a couple of people to observe, perhaps a married couple. Note how the guy is talking to his wife or girlfriend. Note the energy of his hand movements. See how his eyes flash. Note the force of his voice.

Next, imagine he's angry with the woman. Invent angry thoughts and words for him. See how well they go with his voice, his facial expressions, his body language. Then, close your eyes for a minute. Open your eyes, and look at him again. This time imagine he is excited about a new business project. Invent happy, exhilarating thoughts and words for him. Note how well they go with his voice and gestures. Then, go through the same procedure imagining he is frightened because the woman's jealous husband is looking for him.

If you seriously do this exercise just once, you will see how easily you are able to project your thoughts on the facial expressions, tone of voice, and body language of others. This habit is ubiquitous. A work colleague of mine once told me he had spent the entire day thinking I was angry with him. When I told him my dour face was caused by a toothache, he felt relieved.

When others around you appear unhappy, they may be thinking about a thousand things you're not privy to. Maybe they're stewing in some self-worth issues. Or perhaps they're wrestling with anxiety over having to see the dentist. Maybe they're having sexual bondage fantasies. Who knows? I guarantee you — *you* don't have an inkling. The fact is, the other party probably has trouble reading his or her own mind. Don't forget this book is an effort to probe unverbalized attitudes people hold but are unaware of. How will you manage to tune in on the thoughts of somebody who can't discern much of his or her own thinking?

When did you stop beating your wife?

This is sometimes called *the fallacy of many questions* because it conceals one or more additional questions. A prosecutor might ask the defendant, 'Where did you hide the murder weapon?' This improper question veils at least one other question and answer. First, it assumes the defendant has been asked the question, 'Did you murder the victim?' Second, it assumes the defendant has answered *yes* to the invisible question. An alert attorney would leap to his feet and demand the question be divided. I admit I've never seen Perry Mason do this, but there were times when I think he should have.

The fallacy of many questions (also called the fallacy of complex question) often comes on the heels of mind reading. Anxious Annie is having coffee with her boyfriend, Tom. He's trying to prove a point to Annie regarding a political disagreement they are having. Annie suddenly turns on him and says, 'Why are you trying to put me down? Do you always have to prove me wrong?' Tom looks at her blankly. He has no idea what Annie is talking about. But then, he isn't privy to her dotty self-talk.

Annie's self-talk went something like this: *I wonder why he's making such an issue of this? Is he trying to prove something? It seems like he's trying to put me down. The more I think about it, that's exactly what he's up to. Why is he doing this?*

Irrational behaviour usually follows irrational thinking, so the next step is predictable: she angrily lashes out at poor unsuspecting Tom. Tom is dumbfounded. He instinctively knows the question is fallacious, but he doesn't know how to answer. The result is a knock-down, no-win fight.

I say no-win fight because mental fallacies usually hide the real issue. The real problem gets pushed aside as the two parties go at each other hammer and tongs. Tom complains, 'But I'm not trying to put you down.' Annie yells, 'You are too.' She's not ready to brook any disagreement. She has discussed the matter in her own mind and has decided exactly what Tom is thinking and doing. She has fixed her focus tenaciously on *why* Tom is trying to diminish her self-worth, not whether he is, or is not, trying to put her down. That's the bad part about this fallacy — it usually leaves the basic question and answer hidden and unresolved. That's why this ploy is not allowed in proper courtroom questioning.

Annie's hidden self-talk is a highly frustrating puzzle for Tom, who doesn't fully understand what's going on. He knows Annie is being unjust, but he can't pinpoint the problem. Tom accuses Annie of being unfair.

Things often go from bad to worse. As he focuses on her obvious unfairness, he begins to recollect other instances of her unfairness. He starts bringing them up to prove his point. A quiet, enjoyable moment of togetherness has suddenly been turned into a war zone.

Have you ever been guilty of using this fallacy in your self-talk? Do you ever mentally ask yourself questions, answer them, and then proceed to a second question based on the hurriedly dismissed question and answer? I'll bet you all the vodka in Russia you've done this many times. As fallible thinkers, we all do this from time to time. So be alert. Check out the evidence underlying every question and answer played out in your thoughts before moving forward with your train of thought.

⬤ Hasty generalization

Hasty generalization often goes hand-in-hand with low frustration tolerance. Mournful Morrie lost his job and had to go looking for work. He applied for a job at three companies. When none of the three offered him a position, he told himself, 'I figured that would happen. I knew I wouldn't be hired. This certainly proves it. I'll never get anywhere.'

When Morrie decided to take tennis lessons, he did poorly in his first couple of lessons. So he quit. He told himself, 'That taught me a lesson. I just don't have the coordination for sports.' When Morrie is at a party or dance, he always asks just one woman to dance. If she says no, Morrie gives up. One woman's rejection is proof *no* woman will dance with him.

As you can see, Morrie often decides he can't succeed on the basis of one or two failures. Often a single failure is unassailable proof he can't do X. Of course, it's *possible* he'll never succeed at X. But it's not *probable*. Probability factors are not generated on the basis of two or three trials. Probability is built up or lowered with many, many trials.

Even when you have failed many times, you may succeed on the very next effort. Learning occurs on a series of platforms. At the beginning of a platform, you may experience many failures. At the other end of the platform, you may need only one small effort to succeed. Adopt a stubborn gambler's patience. Tell yourself that your next try at X may be the one that succeeds.

If you're prone to making hasty generalizations, remember that mistakes are a part of learning. If you make no mistakes, you are not learning X — you already know how to perform X. Suppose you wanted to learn how to play tennis. On your first visit to the courts, you happen to meet Serena Williams. Let's suppose she takes a liking to you and offers to give you a few tips. Further suppose that you go out on the court with her and easily beat her three sets in a row.

Now think about it. Would you be learning to play tennis? Would anybody accept it if you said, *Gosh, I don't know how I beat Serena. After all, I'm just learning.* Nobody would buy such a farfetched claim. You obviously are able to play superb tennis. How it is that you can play so well, we don't know. Maybe a fairy godmother gave you instant skill. The point I'm driving at is that we learn through failing. When we succeed, we have already learned. A person who never fails at anything in life is learning little and growing less.

Now let's move on to Chapter 9, which is dedicated to what is possibly the most poignant fallacy of all.

9

Why Am I Here?

6 It is enough that we set out to mould the motley stuff
of life into some form of our own choosing; when we
do, the performance is itself the wage. 9

Judge Learned Hand

Several years ago a woman came to one of my support groups feeling depressed. She didn't present any specific problems, but she said she could see no meaning in life. She had been brought up in a religious family, but she no longer considered herself religious. She had rejected theological views on the meaning of life, and she kept asking herself, 'Why am I here? What's the point of it all? Why go on living?' This poignant sense of being adrift with no purpose or direction is a common lament. My heart goes out to those who feel this way; nonetheless, I categorically reject the nonsense it is based on.

To put some light on how I attack this twaddle, I've written an imaginary dialogue between a client and me. It's based on many such conversations I've had with confused members of support groups. As you will see, most moaning and groaning about the purpose of life is based on verbal flimflam.

A Franklinatic journey into the meaning of life

Sally: *Mr. Franklin, I just can't see any purpose to life. What's the point of it? I keep wondering why I'm here on earth.*

Franklin: *The answer is rather simple if you think about it. Your father had sex with your mother. His sperm fertilized an egg. Cells started multiplying. Eventually foetal hormones sent a signal to your mother, and voila: you entered the world.*

Sally: *But that doesn't answer why I'm here.*

Franklin: *Oh yes it does. Suppose you were to ask me why iron rusts. Suppose I told you when oxygen and iron combine they produce iron oxide. You'd accept that as an explanation, wouldn't you?*

Sally: *No, I wouldn't. That only tells me how, not why.*

Franklin: *I think you're playing games with words. What other explanation could I offer you? By explaining how, I do explain why.*

Sally: *Okay, let me word it differently. I guess I want to know what the ultimate purpose of life is.*

Franklin: *Great. Now we're getting somewhere. Let's take a minute to consider the word 'purpose.' Sometimes we have to stop and take a good look at the words we're using when we ask these grandiose questions about life. In other words, you have to understand exactly what it is you're asking. What about this word 'purpose'? Basically it refers to intention. Intention, in turn, implies consciousness. Consider a simple example. I go to the store because I'm out of milk. We say my intention is to buy a carton of milk. We can stretch this meaning to cover not only what we do, but also to cover what we make. When primitive man carved a bowl out of stone, he intended it to be used for food. Without this conscious purpose behind the* *making of an artifact, we could not properly use the term 'purpose'. Suppose we find a stone hollowed out by water and erosion. Suppose this stone is almost identical to one hollowed out by an ancient cave dweller. We would not say the stone hollowed out by water had the purpose of holding food. An archaeologist would only describe a stone hollowed out by human hand as having such a purpose.*

What I'm trying to tell you is that the word purpose implies a **purposer***.*

Sally: *What does all this playing with words have to do with why I'm here?*

Franklin: *Don't you see? What you long for is a great Purposer who will give your life purpose or intention. For, without a purposer, there can be no purpose.*

Sally: *You're making me sound superstitious. I definitely am not looking for magical forces hovering over me and directing my life.*

Franklin: *Nonetheless, your question may be an unconscious effort to slip something supernatural in through the back door. If you don't believe some purposer intends that you do certain things with your life, your question has been fully answered by my original answer. Your parents copulated, sperm fertilized an egg, and so on.*

Sally: *Okay, I get the point. But what about questions such as, 'What's the purpose of the heart'? Surely that's not a meaningless question.*

Franklin: *You're absolutely right. It's a valid question, but your new question is valid only because you've coyly changed the meaning of the word 'purpose'. You see, 'purpose' is also used to mean function. Your question could easily be phrased as, 'What's the function of the heart?' My answer, of course, would be, 'The function of the heart is to pump blood.'*

	Surely you'll agree this answers the question. If I give you a scientific explanation of how the heart works and what it does, I also explain why you have a heart. What other explanation could I possibly give?
Sally:	*Now I think I understand what you're driving at. My original question, 'Why am I here?' is a fake. If I were honest, I would ask something like, 'Are there magical forces directing my life?' And if so, what do these magical forces intend for me?*
Franklin:	*Exactly. Now I want you to pause and think about how appropriate these questions are for you.*
Sally:	*I see your point. Since I'm not a superstitious person, such questions are not suitable.*
Franklin:	*Now you're getting somewhere. The next thing to consider is whether a question makes sense. Your original question is illogical. It conceals an ancient fallacy called the fallacy of many questions. This trickery is used to hide a previous question and its answer. In your case, the hidden question is, 'Are there magical forces or a purposer giving my life purpose?' You have assumed a yes answer to this question and then gone on to ask yourself what that purpose is.*
Sally:	*But I feel sad and empty when I think of my life as having no purpose.*
Franklin:	*Then give it purpose. Since it's your life, you are its purposer. Just assign a purpose to your life. It's that simple. State what your goals are. These become the purpose of your life.*

Following this session, Sally refocused her energies on other subjects and made great progress in dealing with her sense of ennui. She embraced my suggestion and made happiness and healthy survival her two most important goals. Her sense of being directionless soon evaporated.

You would do well to emulate Sally. Suppose you choose the goals of happiness and healthy survival. These would be your long-term goals in life. Of course, in order to reach those goals, you would also need some short-term goals. These are the vehicles that carry you toward your ultimate goals. Together these sets of goals give your life direction.

Don't you agree it's more useful to pick goals than to sit around whining about how meaningless life is? I urge you to do three things:

1. Decide what you want from life.
2. Decide how to best get it.
3. Then act.

Does this seem simplistic or glib? Could one simply decide to make happinss a goal in life? Dr Harold Greenwald has developed a whole system of therapy based on the belief that a person actually can make such decisions. He found that many of his clients had at some time in their lives made the decision to be unhappy. He began showing them they could just as easily choose to be happy. He calls his unusual approach *decision therapy*. Dr Greenwald claims he has had excellent results with this method. I say you have nothing to lose by adopting this approach. Decide to be happy. Then go for it.

Just make sure this decision, or any other choice, is not prompted by the voices of authority. Make the operative decisions in your life *your* decisions. And start making them now. If you're acting as though life is all work and no play, you can decide to work less and play more. If you're tired of doing much for others and little for yourself, you can decide to indulge yourself more often. Take no notice if some guru tells you the purpose of your life is to serve others.

Remember, you are the only person in the universe who knows what the purpose of your life is because you, and only you, choose that purpose. There is no purpose to life *per se*. You are the great Purposer of your own life. That purpose consists of the goals *you* assign to your life. When some famous person pontificates on what the purpose of life is, he or she is merely passing gas.

If you believe X is true because some pedagogue (or dema-
gogue) says so, you are yielding to the ancient fallacy of *ipse
dixit* — he said so, therefore it must be true. In other words,
don't believe everything you hear, especially in the area of self-
help. When it comes to the world of pop psychology, I suggest
you disbelieve half of what you hear and strongly doubt the
other half. This is a field where rational scepticism may save
your emotional life.

You will hear conflicting claims from peers, teachers, doctors,
gurus, rabbis, priests, parents, colleagues, shrinks and a host of
modern-day witch doctors. As you confront this tower of gabble,
never lose sight of the fact that you are the only authority on the
purpose of your life.

So far, I've only talked about the meaning of *purpose*. But if
we're going to talk about the purpose of life, we also had best
look at the meaning of the word 'life'. Life is a physical and
mental process. It metabolizes, grows, reproduces, reacts to stim-
uli, and so forth. Life is basically an energy-changing flow that
ends with death.

So why do some people insist this process must have
meaning? Is there some hidden true meaning I'm missing?
Frankly, I doubt it. Even if there is such a meaning, it appears to
be unknowable. All we know is that one's life process can be
used as we choose to use it. Think of your life as a tool. The
meaning or purpose of a tool does not lie in the tool itself — its
purpose lies in how you choose to use it.

So simply make a decision as to how you will use this vital
process while it lasts. Although heredity and environment
impose real limits, a given life process has many latent potentials. You can work to achieve all or none of these potentials, or
you can work to enhance specific potentials. This is not to say
you must fulfil any of your potentials. As a matter of fact, insisting that you must fulfil specific potentials can lead you into
neurotic perfectionism or slavery to your work. It actually may
be in your best interest to settle for less ambitious goals.

This whole business of *living up to one's potential* is tricky.
Mournful Morrie, for example, often frets about falling short of

his potential. His self-talk has thoughts such as, *I'm just not living up to my potential. I've wasted my life. What a failure I am. I'm never going to get anywhere.* And so on. This self-talk script is riddled with claptrap, but I want to focus mainly on the word *potential.*

Never forget that we live in an orderly universe. Scientifically speaking, events only happen when they *should* happen, and they can only happen the way they *do* happen. When all the necessary conditions are present, an event will, must and should occur. If you fail your maths exam, you have achieved exactly what you should achieve. All the conditions necessary for you to fail the exam were present. If that were not the case, you wouldn't have failed the exam.

> Never forget that we live in an orderly universe.

What I'm saying is that you always fulfil *some* potential. And that potential is exactly the one you *should* fulfil. When you worry about realizing your potential, you're playing a guessing game. You're guessing at what you can achieve. It's true your guess may be an educated one based on past performance, but there is always a new configuration of variables present for each event of your life. Often you are not aware of new variables that have entered the scene to play a role. If you are merely guessing about your future achievements in a new arena, your guess will be even more unreliable.

Guessing aside, people who worry about their potentials usually are should-ing on themselves. Their self-talk is filled with musturbation. *I must, I should, I ought to, I have to achieve X.* If they fail to achieve X, and thereby fail to live up to their 'potential', they label themselves failures. This is a bad habit if ever there was one. Why treat yourself so unkindly?

Morrie often calls himself a washout when he sees himself falling short of his mythical potential. The odd thing is that Morrie would never do that to a friend. He would never say to his buddy George, *George, I think you're a failure, an utter washout. You haven't even come close to your potential.* Yet he cruelly says these kinds of things to himself. Are you guilty of this? Don't you think this is a little odd?

I referred to Morrie's so-called potential as 'mythical' because the concept is a reification. Whenever we talk about things in the future, we are essentially reifying. The future itself is a reification. It's not some place we can visit or locate or film. One's potential is not a *thing* we can see, touch, hear, or photograph, so be careful with this word *potential*. Don't glibly scatter it throughout your self-talk.

In any case, who's to say that realizing one's so-called potential is always a good thing? Suppose you had the potential to be a great embezzler or a skilled contract killer. Do you think you should try to fulfil these potentials? And even if the potential is something highly valued in our society, *must* you strive to realize that alleged capacity? Suppose you had the potential to be a great ballet dancer or a business tycoon. Who says you have to become a fabulous dancer or a financial giant?

Don't swallow this twaddle. We tend to become immersed in endless social bromides and wearisome platitudes. If a youngster decides to drop out of college, the parents have a nervous breakdown. Mom and Dad horribilize, beat their breasts and vociferously should on their children. It's true that finishing college is usually in one's best interest. But it also may be in one's best interest to drop out and become an electrician or open a toy store. And even if such choices are not in one's best interest, what law of the universe says we must always do what's in our so-called best interest?

By all means, try to make rational decisions; but when you slip and make eccentric or clearly dumb decisions, accept the consequences and get on with the business of living.

As a final note, never let your guard down with regard to the myth of self-worth. It will hover over every enterprise you undertake, over all your self-counselling, over your every aspiration, over every personal relationship, over all the crucial decisions of your life. Whatever you look for, whatever you seek in life, whatever you pursue, make sure you are not being governed by this most pernicious of all human myths.

10

Trekking Toward a New World View

6 The man who never alters his opinions is like standing water, and breeds reptiles of the mind. 9

William Blake

With all this talk about control and science and logic, you may wonder if I've been bent upon turning you into an emotionless robot. Absolutely not. A major goal of rational self-talk is to make room for positive, fulfilling emotions by better containing negative emotions. It's anger that crowds out love. It's depression that shuts out the beauty around us. It's fear that blocks journeys of growth. When we conquer these destructive emotions, we don't shape an emotionless void — we create new space we can fill with more love, more awareness of beauty, and more courage to walk down new roads.

Think about it: you can't ever be completely emotionless. You are always in *some* emotional state — be it peace or excitement. What you don't want is a set of negative emotions that run wild. To be happy, you need a system to tame your emotion-brain and make it subservient to your goals in life. Perhaps you want to lose weight, overcome jealousy, be more active, end an affair, write a novel, change jobs, stop smoking, learn to dance, find a mate, stop procrastinating, or go back to college. Do you have any of these goals? Are you spinning your wheels? If so, you are likely mired in irrational self-talk.

Remember, your emotion-brain often works blindly, unwittingly dragging you down as you reach for your goals. Dummibrain will buy any bill of goods you send him. It doesn't matter whether it's a contradiction or a gross exaggeration. The voice of your thinking brain is a voice from a burning bush, and Dummibrain believes with simple faith. Credulity, not scepticism, is the hallmark of your old brain. The messages you send to this primitive brain must be cautiously crafted.

Dummibrain is not equipped to run your life — at least not in a modern society. Your thinking brain must stay in the saddle if you want to grow and realize your dreams. Only your new brain has the capacity to see clearly and steer you through the maze of obstacles we face in life. Dummibrain is more likely to run you head first into a brick wall, leaving you bloodied and none the wiser as to how or why you cracked your head.

This doesn't mean your left brain is a paragon of rationality. It merely has the capacity to use logic and evidence. Alas, even our thinking brain believes all sorts of bunkum. This is because many of our irrational beliefs are shaped when we are children, a time in life when we're intellectually naïve. During these callow years, we're bombarded with an extravagant amount of rubbish from parents, peers, school, church and television. We unthinkingly adopt this hokum and go on to practise it for years until it hardens into attitudinal automatism.

As adults, we mindlessly adhere to a host of senseless beliefs as though they were laws of the universe. Many of these long-practised beliefs are powerful shibboleths in our society, so I urge you to adopt a feisty scepticism as we challenge a whole herd of these sacred cows. We are all to some degree culture-bound, but reason asks us to break those shackles that constrict our growth.

Try to imagine the jeers early astronomers suffered when they declared the world was round. The idea sounded preposterous, perhaps as absurd as some of my claims sound to you. But remember this: no belief is above being questioned when it fails the tests of logic and evidence. What is truly foolhardy is to continue believing something irrespective of whether it is true or not.

You may wonder whether you can shed some of your deepest beliefs, especially those dating to your childhood. I assure you that you can. The false conviction that you can't do this comes from the notion that ideas are implanted in a child's mind and that they then live on with a life of their own. The fact is we choose to maintain these beliefs as adults. We systematically nurture all sorts of nonsense with our self-talk. We repeatedly tell ourselves the same old drivel day after day, year after year.

We can, however, choose otherwise. Many children are inculcated with the religion of their parents; yet, when they reach adulthood, they rethink and then reject the religion they were raised in. Some are raised in puritanical families but join nudist camps as adults. Some are raised in military families, but join pacifist groups as adults. The examples are legion.

Let's look at an example suggested by Dr Maxie Maultsby. As a child, you probably believed in Santa Claus. Do you remember how you constructed your belief? If you think about it, there were three stages to the growth of your belief.

During stage one, you gathered evidence. You saw that gifts mysteriously appeared under the Christmas tree overnight. You saw that Santa's cookies had been eaten. And, of course, you went to a store or mall and actually visited Santa. Second, you started acting on your belief. You wrote letters to Santa. You hung out your stocking. You left out cookies for Santa on Christmas Eve. In stage three, your belief came to feel natural. Your belief in Santa had become an integral part of your world view. This stage is akin to the feeling an American living in England for a long time finally has as he drives down the left side of a British road.

Now try to remember how you changed your belief. This came in four stages. First, you started noticing counterevidence. You noticed a Santa on every downtown street corner. You wondered how Santa could possibly visit every kid in the world on Christmas Eve. You found one of your gifts from Santa in the cupboard a week before Christmas. Second, you devised a new explanation for where your gifts came from. You suspected your parents bought them. Third, you started acting on your new belief. You stopped writing letters to Santa and visiting him at the department store and putting out cookies. Then, in the fourth and last stage, you came to feel comfortable with your new belief. Your new ideational shoes, so to speak, had been broken in.

This is the same method you will use to change your current dysfunctional beliefs. You will use new information and logic to challenge an old notion. You will generate a new belief based on logic and facts. You will start using this belief in your self-talk. Soon, you will be acting on your new thoughts. Eventually, they will feel more natural than your old beliefs.

As you begin this process of unseating your old irrational beliefs, you will find that many of them occur in little clusters. These are scripts you've rehearsed for years, sentence clusters you predictably use in specific situations. For example, you may have a long-practised script you use when you get a parking ticket, or your work is criticized, or you're rejected by a lover.

These learned scripts have the imprint of your personal style. You may be a *what-iffer*. When your supervisor nitpicks over your work, you may say such things as *She sounds angry. What if I don't get that promotion I've been depending on? Worse yet, what if she fires me? What if I get behind on my house payments and lose the house? Oh God, what if my wife leaves me?*

Another common style is that of *should-ing*. If you're a *should-er*, you might say something like *Hell's bells, my boss shouldn't talk that way to me. She should realize she didn't give me enough time to polish my report. She shouldn't pick on my work when her own work is nothing to rave about. She should show more respect.*

A third common cognitive style is that of the self-downer. This person says such things as *Oh, God! I screwed up again. I never do anything right. I'm always messing up. I'll never amount to anything. I guess I just don't have what it takes.* Some self-downers go beyond this silent self-talk, and we actually hear them saying these things out loud.

Of course, it's easier if you identify your cognitive style before you attempt to attack it. This is not easy, but the benefits are great. Defining your dominant self-talk has some big advantages. Let's say you find that certain anger-provoking sentences keep appearing in your thoughts whenever you have to stand in line at the supermarket. As you attack these nutty thoughts and work to rewrite this script, you'll also be working toward defusing your anger in similar situations. As you improve the self-talk you use in a grocery line, you will improve the self-talk you use when stuck in a traffic jam. As the rising anger you feel in the grocery line is blocked by your new self-talk, the rising anger you feel in traffic jams will become easier to block.

As you go about identifying and rewriting your crazy scripts, you'll be getting at something deeper: you'll be unmasking a world view. Take the what-iffer. He has a *possibilistic* world view. He compulsively looks at countless possibilities as though they were realities. He fails to understand that his thoughts are merely possibilities engendered by an unbridled imagination. He's convinced that many of his envisioned disasters are soon-to-be realities. This is a basic way of looking at the world he has probably practised for years. Of course, it's a highly superstitious view of reality.

Fortunately, if he works hard and creates rational self-talk, this underlying orientation will change. He will begin to look at life on the basis of probabilities. He will shift from a superstitious world view to a rational view of life and its perils. His world view will become *probabilistic* — an outlook that will no longer hamstring him in working toward his goals or enjoying life.

This kind of reprogramming can also prevent an explosion of secondary problems. Suppose you're overweight. Further suppose you incite Dummibrain into pulling your depression lever. This means you now have two problems instead of one: you are overweight *and* depressed. Alas, the eruption of new problems may only be starting. You may eat more to elevate your mood. This leads to a third problem: you gain more weight. This, in turn, is worsened because depression tends to immobilize you, and that keeps you from exercising. And this leads to... As you can see, your problems can mushroom at an amazing rate. A single problem can give rise to 20. And all because of looney self-talk.

Most of the time dotty self-talk is simply illogical or lacking evidence to support it. But sometimes it's a matter of poor focus. Take the example of the *yes-but* habit. We might call this the *sitting-on-your-backside* habit. Or you might call it the *going-through-life-but-first* habit. Whatever you choose to call it, it's a hurtful mental proclivity.

Let me illustrate how this could interfere with getting the most out of this book. As you read these pages, suppose you were to keep saying things such as *Yes, but I don't know if that applies to me. Yes, but I don't think that would be realistic for me. Yes, but who has time to do that? Yes, but Franklin isn't taking into account...* Do you think this verbal habit would be helpful to you?

So how do you get off your *but*? Simple: just concentrate on the *yes* part of your sentences. Whenever you hear yourself saying yes, but..., forget about what comes after *but* and focus on the agreement reflected in your *yes*. Saying *yes* means you basically agree. Adding a *but* seldom adds anything useful. Often the *but* part of the sentence does three things: (1) it dampens your motivation, (2) it creates a prejudice in your mind, and (3) it serves as a cop-out.

More often than not this habit is mere nitpicking that distracts you from your real problem. In addition, the *yes, but* habit may reflect low esteem on your part. You may use it to build your own importance by cutting down the virtues of others. Listen to a *yes-butter* in a conversation: You say, 'Sally is very witty.' The yes-butter answers, 'Yes, but she dresses so tacky.' You say, 'Henry is very thoughtful.' The yes-butter answers, 'Yes, but he's so boring.' Do you see how ugly this habit is? And do you see how it can close your mind to positive realities? Not to mention the way it broadcasts your own feelings of inferiority.

What I'm saying is that you may read these pages with cognitive filters that impede what you get out of the book. You face an odd paradox in that you should have read this book before reading this book in order to get the most out of this book. It's likely you're mostly reading it for interest or enjoyment on your first trip through these pages. If so, I urge you to read the entire book a second time, focusing on it as a serious guide to mental-emotional growth. After one reading, you'll just be starting to get tuned into your self-talk habits. With your new insights, you'll be less likely to undermine the potential benefits to be found in this system of self-counselling. Having seen the forest, you will be better able to take measure of the trees.

Another reason for reading this little volume at least twice is the need to hammer yourself with repetition. You will need to uncover and debunk dozens of self-talk mistakes. You will need to create and memorize scores of new sentences. Your new self-talk must become as automatic as the bunkum you've been telling yourself for years. This means reading and rereading, thinking and rethinking, learning and relearning. Think of it as something akin to learning tennis. In tennis you have to study and practise your forehand over and over again. Then you have to analyze and practise your serve over and over again. And so forth.

This means work and hard work and more hard work. With so much effort, you'll certainly want to see some progress. After all, you wouldn't want to go on a diet for several months and then find you still weigh the same according to the scales. So how are you going to measure your progress?

Dr Paul Hauck suggests three indicators of rational-emotive progress: (1) frequency (2) duration and (3) intensity. Suppose you lose your temper ten times daily. That's frequency. Suppose each time you make yourself anxious, you stay fearful for an hour. That's duration. As for intensity, it's something you'll feel in your body, and it's not easily measured without a battery of instruments; nonetheless, you'll have a strong awareness of certain physical feelings going up or down as you become cognizant of how you upset or calm yourself.

A word of caution: you can easily discourage yourself if you irrationally use these yardsticks. Make a strong effort to maintain realistic goals. Take the matter of frequency. Let's suppose you have a hot temper you want to work on. Let's say you keep a log and find you're blowing your fuse an average of ten times daily. Suppose that after one month of hard work, you find you're averaging nine temper tantrums daily. This might trigger a temper tantrum in itself, and you might write me a letter telling me what a charlatan I am. By doing so, you would be committing an either-or fallacy.

Think about it carefully. It takes you one month to go from ten to nine tantrums. If you maintain this rate of progress, you will completely eliminate a destructive habit in only ten months. People go to school for years to learn a trade or profession. Others lift weights for years to reshape their bodies. Mountain climbers prepare for years just to climb one mountain.

Would it be worth it to you to spend ten months unlearning a hurtful habit? Take a long-term view. Don't foolishly discount what seem like small bits of progress. Give yourself a pat on the back for every scintilla of improvement.

Take another example. Suppose you are an extremely shy young man who has trouble talking to women. You study this book for several weeks. You work hard to identify and replace the self-talk blocking your efforts to meet women. Finally, on a Sunday afternoon at the park, you actually manage to cautiously strike up a conversation with a woman you've never seen before. Encouraged, you work even harder to improve your self-talk and thereby overcome your irrational fear of approaching women. The next weekend, you manage to talk to two new women in the park. At this rate, by the end of the year, you would be talking to 52 new women every weekend. Nobody would accuse you of being shy. Of being a compulsive Don Juan, maybe — but definitely not shy.

Rating your progress is also made tricky by virtue of the seesaw ideational contest going on in your head. You don't simply disarm a battery of screwy beliefs and then usher in, unopposed, a new platoon of rational beliefs. The old ideas are cagey. They merely beat a temporary retreat as you press forward with your new beliefs. You may think the old nutty ideas are vanquished, but they usually continue to lurk and lie in wait.

This means you will go through an indefinite period of holding opposing beliefs simultaneously. At least, it will seem that way. Sometimes the old beliefs will hold sway. Other times, your new self-talk will win the day. You'll know which beliefs are in the saddle mainly by how you feel and act. If you feel anxious before giving that talk to the PTA, you're using your old self-talk hokum. If you feel calm, you're using your new rational beliefs.

This seesaw clash of beliefs means you'll often take two steps forward and one step backward. During stressful times, you may even take one step forward and two steps back. Don't let that throw you. It's to be expected. As soon as you make some progress and get ahead in the game, you'll tend to coast for a while. When you let your guard down, your old irrational self-talk comes out of hiding and takes over. Don't worry when this happens. You can quickly recoup your losses and reimpose rational self-talk. Shepherding your emotion-brain is a skill. And, like most skills, it's easier to call it back into service than to start from scratch. So don't dump on yourself when you backslide. Look at the average rate of progress over many months. Forget about perfection.

Keep reminding yourself you are not a god. You are an imperfect mortal. As a fallible human being, you will necessarily stumble as you try to set up new lines of communication with your emotion-brain.

> **Keep reminding yourself you are not a god.**

Like a toddler, you'll be wobbly and awkward. Sometimes you'll fall flat on your face. Try to take these pratfalls with a sense of humour. Simply get back on your feet, dust off your rear, and go stumbling back down the road. You won't, of course, ever reach the end of your journey — at least, if that end is perfection in the management of your emotions. You will, however, go a long way toward taking control of your life. Not without bruises, of course. But they will only be bruises, not the cutting wounds inflicted by irrational self-talk. You will feel the ache of leaving your old ways, but the pain of changing is far, far less than the pain of remaining immobilized while your brief stay on Earth passes you by.

11

The Three Stages of Learning

6 In Endymion, I leaped headlong into the Sea, and thereby have become better acquainted with the quicksands and the rocks, than if I had stayed upon the green shore, and piped a silly pipe, and took tea, and comfortable advice. I was never afraid of failure... 9

John Keats

Before sending you on your way to practise your new self-talk scripts, I want to caution you about some of the pitfalls that can trip you up at each stage of your learning if you aren't prepared for them.

In general terms, you must bear in mind that as you embark on trying out your new scripts and begin to act in different ways, you'll often feel tugged in other directions. No question about it, your new thoughts and actions will often feel awkward and unnatural. But once again, I must admonish you: *do not trust your feelings.* Just keep reminding yourself that one day your new ways will feel more natural than your old ways. Keep in mind the example of an American tourist in England trying to drive on the left side of the road. Your journey will cause you similar feelings of discomfort.

I want you to keep in mind that the new you won't emerge as a single event. As you practise your new thoughts and self-talk, you will go through three distinct learning stages. The first stage is what I call the postmortem stage. At this level of skill you're just beginning to see how it is you upset yourself with dotty self-talk. Suppose you've had a bad day at the office, and on the way home you get a flat tyre. You step out of your car, take one look at your pancaked tyre, and fire off a series of curses directed at your car, your job, and the world in general. This, of course, is attentively listened to by Dummibrain. He instantly takes over your actions, and you deliver a mighty kick to your wheel. Ouch. Now you have a sprained toe. Two problems instead of one.

Later that day, with your toe soaking in Epsom salts, you recall your temper tantrum. You think about what you said to yourself. Suddenly a light bulb goes on. You spot several irrational shoulds imbedded in your lingering Jehovah complex. You have an *Aha!* reaction as you zero in on the squirrely self-talk that led to your temper tantrum.

This is a critical point for you. You can take two paths at this juncture. One of them is to dump on yourself for being 'stupid' and using self-talk you know is hurtful. Don't do this. It will sink you by torpedoing your motivation. Instead, tell yourself, *Hey, I'm making some real progress. I'm beginning to see what it is I do wrong. Until now, I've never been able to figure out why I become so mad over such little frustrations. At last I'm getting some insight.* That is the kind of self-talk that will: (1) make you feel better, (2) spur you on to work harder and (3) give you more practice in penetrating your relations with Dummibrain.

The second stage is the most exasperating. By the time you've reached this level, you've managed to compress your time frame. Now you're able to see what you're doing at the exact moment you're doing it. At the very instant you're relaying a self-defeating message to your emotion-brain, you become aware of what you're doing. This, however, doesn't deter you. You relentlessly forge ahead with your destructive self-talk. You see clearly what you're doing, but you seem to be a helpless spectator watching your own self-abuse.

This can give you an urge to put yourself down. After all, haven't you been sitting there like a nincompoop watching yourself foolishly stirring up a storm in your emotion-brain? Fight this self-blame if you want to stay motivated. Tell yourself something like this: *Hey, I've made it to the second stage. It's just like Franklin said it would be. I can actually tune in on my nutty ideas at the very moment I'm using them. Now I can really unleash a counterattack on some of the hogwash I tell myself.*

You will no doubt find this stage highly annoying, but it beats postmortems in that you'll now start to see some modest improvements in how you feel and behave.

Finally, if you persevere, you'll reach the third and last stage. This stage is as exciting as the second level is annoying. At this point in your progress, you're able to sense it when you're about to fire off an irrational message to Dummibrain. You're able to anticipate your own self-talk. Almost at the moment you send your usual claptrap to Dummibrain, you set up a roadblock and your faulty self-talk is stopped in its tracks.

Much to your amazement, you remain calm and self-assured in the face of severe frustration. It is at this point that you are truly taking control of your emotional life. The reason is simple: at this stage you have seriously weakened your faulty self-talk, and you are beginning to replace it with rational thoughts. This in turn is giving you a degree of serenity in the face of adversity that you never thought possible. I promise you, you will feel exhilarated at this triumphal moment.

Alas, such moments probably will not come if you read this book only once. I must caution you once again to read it at least two times, perhaps even three or four times. Many readers of this book have followed this advice and have written to me to say they got much more out of the book the second time around. During your second reading, many seemingly disconnected ideas will come together as a whole. Some concepts are not easily absorbed with only one reading. Consider that few readers fully grasp the difference between rational shoulds and irrational shoulds on their first reading of the chapter on the Jehovah complex. I know from experience as a counsellor that this concept takes considerable thought and reflection before it fully sinks in.

Furthermore, backsliding is common among those who practise rational self-counselling. It's like brushing your teeth. If you don't do it religiously every day, you may find yourself rapidly sliding back into your old ways. One reader told me he was on his sixth reading of this book. He considers it a form of mental hygiene as vital to be followed as one's oral hygiene. I'm not suggesting you go that far, but a second reading is definitely in order. As I've already said, this book needs to be read before it is read.

In a way, I envy the journey you're about to take toward a new world view. If you hold to the course, it could become the most exciting experience of your life. The key is to tenaciously persist when seemingly stuck on any given learning platform. And yes, you will often fall down. Big deal. Pick yourself up and write it off as a necessary pratfall due to the fact that you're a fallible human being. Walk down the path I've laid out, and I promise you the rewards will more than justify the trek.

12

On Being Your Own Counsellor

❝ Every tub must stand on its own bottom. **❞**

Thomas Fuller

Many mental health professional snigger at self-help books. Their sneers, however, will not change the facts. History is filled with examples of people who have had their lives changed by a single book. Books are entries into the greatest minds of history. As such, they are priceless sources of information for the person embarking on a programme of self-growth. Which do you suppose would be better: a rational self-counselling programme guided by the books of Albert Ellis? Or going through rebirthing with some New Age Hollywood counsellor?

Keep in mind that all effective psychotherapy is ultimately a process of self-help. A counsellor can guide the process, but the person seeking change must ultimately use the information he is given to revamp his dysfunctional thinking. He must, in other words, sit on his own bottom.

I don't want to you to be isolated from other sources of rational self-counselling guidance. Dr Albert Ellis, for example, strongly recommends using what he calls *bibliotherapy*. This is simply the reading of rational self-help books as an adjunct to your self-counselling. In fact, Dr Ellis has written an impressive number of books for just that purpose, and these books have helped millions of people around the world to better their lives.

History clearly abounds with examples of people who have dramatically changed their lives after reading a single book. Stuart Chase pored for months over *Science and Sanity* by Alfred Korzybski. Chase was enraptured by the new windows it opened to his understanding of himself and the world. Musing over this experience, he would later write, *To one who reads and reflects patiently upon this book, the world can never look as it did before. It moves nearer. Many things which were once blurred and misty come into focus.*

My favourite case history of how powerful bibliotherapy can be is that of Raymond. This middle-aged bachelor was working for a large West Coast corporation. Raymond had been handicapped by a lifelong problem with anger. When Raymond was driving to and from work, for example, if another vehicle cut him off, he would follow it for miles in hopes of exacting revenge. He was having friction with his boss, his colleagues, his secretary and many of his business contacts. His anger was clearly blocking his professional goals, and he wanted to change.

The problem was that Raymond had little faith in the counselling profession — who can blame him? — and he refused to see a therapist. A friend of Raymond's asked me for suggestions. In response, I mailed Raymond a slim book by Paul Hauck, O*vercoming Frustration and Anger.*

At first, Raymond was sceptical, and the book lay untouched for weeks. Then one night, feeling bored and restless, he picked up Hauck's little book and started reading. After one chapter, he was hooked. He did not put it down until he had finished. The next day, he picked it up and read it again. He kept reading and rereading the book until he nearly had it memorized.

This was Raymond's first exposure to rational self-counselling, and he was enchanted by its clarity and good sense. He immediately began using its principles. Within one week, his behaviour at work had changed dramatically. He became calmer, more patient, more reflective. He changed so quickly and so visibly, the corporation gossip mill soon was churning out spurious tales that Raymond was using drugs. Oh well, I guess you can't win them all.

Countless people have changed their lives using another self-help book, *New Guide to Rational Living* by Albert Ellis and Robert Harper. Many clients have told me they became happier after reading and using another fine book written by Dr David Burns, *Feeling Good*. Many thousands of students have used *Overcoming Procrastination* by Albert Ellis to improve their study habits.

Don't let the nabobs of the mental health profession beguile you into believing this is all pie in the sky. You can use this book and many others to change your emotional life. Simply make the decision to do so. Then act.

> **Don't let the nabobs of the mental health profession talk you into believing this is all pie in the sky.**

Simply by reading this far, you have already launched yourself on a programme of self-help. Of course, this is only a first step. I've urged you *ad nauseam* to reread this book at least once. As you read it the second time, take notes, study your notes, maintain a day journal, and talk to others about what you're learning. Spend some time each day improving your scripts. Last, but not least, you should persistently think about your thinking.

I certainly don't want you to make this book the sole or necessarily the primary book for your bibliotherapy. As you master and absorb the concepts in this book, expand your reading. For that, you'll need a few reading suggestions. I've never been fond of bibliographies. After all, how does one choose from so many books? Authors give us long lists of books, but they rarely tell us anything about them. So rather than present you with a meaningless list of titles, I decided to simply provide a chatty description of a few of my favourite self-help books.

The pioneer best-selling book in Rational Self-Counselling is the already mentioned *New Guide to Rational Living* by Albert Ellis and Robert Harper. This book lays out the theory of rational therapy in clear, understandable language. This volume has probably launched more people into rational self-counselling (now called *Rational-Emotive Behaviour Therapy* by Ellis) than any other book. It is still arguably the best book of its kind ever written.

The authors dedicate a chapter to each of the basic irrational ideas human beings are prone to. Included are sets of rational thoughts you can use to replace those particular screwy scripts. You could certainly do worse than start your reading programme with this classic.

One small caution: the book doesn't give much attention to the differences between explicit self-talk and the unverbalized attitudes that quietly skulk on the edge of consciousness. Dr Maxie Maultsby, on the other hand, does a nice job of distinguishing between these two elements of thinking in *Help Yourself to Happiness*. Maultsby, who is a former disciple of Albert Ellis, has branched off and developed what he calls *Rational Behaviour Therapy* to distinguish it from the REBT of Ellis. As far as I can see, the differences are mostly tactical.

Maultsy's book is also useful for learning a technique he calls *rational-emotive imagery*. This is a powerful way to practise your scripts in imaginary settings before you try them in real settings. Many studies have shown such imaging is a potent tool. As you progress in monitoring your self-talk, acquaint yourself with techniques of rational-emotive imagery. Bear in mind that we 'talk' to ourselves with pictures as well as words.

If you're fond of brevity, Gerald Kranzler has written a slim volume I often recommend to first-timers. *You Can Change How You Feel* is only 48 pages long. This makes it easy to reread, a practice I strongly encourage. You can read this book six times in the same time it would take you to read a longer work once. A solid, worthwhile little book.

Do you have problems with anger? I heartily recommend reading the already mentioned *Overcoming Frustration and Anger* by Paul Hauck. Hauck has written a series of small books in the field of rational self-help, but I consider this to be his best book. It is clear, well-organized, and practical. Its brief 142 pages make it easy to read it several times. Hauck has a forceful, no-nonsense approach I like.

If anger is your dominant emotion, you may want to study this destructive emotion further. *Anger: How to Live With and Without It* by Albert Ellis is the deepest and most complete analysis of anger I've read. If you want an in-depth understanding of your anger, you may want to make this your standard reference. Among many topics, Ellis provides a sharply drawn profile of the grandiosity behind anger. Another thing I like about the book is the way Ellis covers a broad range of situations from politics to feminism to non-violence to simple friendship. I periodically revisit this book just to keep my Jehovah complex in check.

Is depression your main problem? If so, try reading *Feeling Good* by David Burns. This is a solid book with little padding. Almost every page has something to offer. Ironically, this is something the book suffers from. It is so packed with advice and exercises, a reader tends to feel overwhelmed. With 400 pages of small print, the book is daunting when it comes to rereading it. I wish Burns had written a series of three or four books to make his materials more manageable. Aside from that minor caveat, this book is probably one of the best self-help books ever written on the subject of depression. To deal with the large number of exercises and tips, choose only a few exercises you like, and master them first.

If you have trouble accepting neurotic hostility in other people, *Feeling Good* has fine techniques for defusing anger in others. My favourite book, however, on coping with irrational behaviour in others is *How To Live With a 'Neurotic' At Home and At Work* by Albert Ellis. I include this book on my ten-best list of rational self-help books. If you feel puzzled by what exactly neurosis is, read this book. Ellis offers one of the most lucid, concise descriptions of neurosis I've read.

This book will be useful to anybody who has to deal with a moody spouse, lover, roommate, neighbour, colleague, boss, secretary, or store clerk. Keep in mind that much emotional disturbance is triggered within the arena of banal, everyday relations with other people. This book will give you some excellent tools for living with our nutty human race. A final tip: if you're worried about reading it around your spouse or roommate, simply find another jacket for the book.

Another book on my ten-best list is *Overcoming Procrastination* by Albert Ellis and William Knaus. I've already mentioned this fine book, but I want to repeat my recommendation. The authors do a wonderful job exploring the issues of self-rating, self-worth, and self-confidence, and one could easily use this as a basic primer in rational self-counselling.

If you're looking for help in developing your assertiveness, Ellis's book on anger has some good tips. My favourite book on this topic, however, is *Responsible Assertive Behaviour* by Arthur Lange and Patricia Jakubowski. This is written for counsellors, but a lay person working on self-counselling can easily profit from reading it. The authors do an especially nice job on separating aggression and assertion.

I've already mentioned *Science and Sanity*, a famous book by Alfred Korzybski that strongly affected the world view of Stuart Chase. Korzybski is the founding father of general semantics. This fascinating school of thought digs into the relationships between language, thought, and emotion. If you delve into general semantics, you will find that it overlaps rational self-counselling in many ways.

If that linkage intrigues you, you might want to tackle *Science and Sanity* in order to deepen your knowledge of general semantics; however, I actually don't recommend tackling this morass of tangled syntax and dense verbosity. Luckily, you can read a much easier introduction to general semantics. Dr SI Hayakawa, a devotee of general semantics, wrote an easy-to-undertand book entitled *Language in Thought and Action*. The second half of this book, in particular, overlaps significantly with what we do in rational self-counselling.

If you study and digest this book, it may profoundly affect your world view. Many people report that they underwent deep changes in their thinking after studying general semantics. The economist Stuart Chase became an ardent spokesperson for general semantics after studying Korzybski. As a matter of fact, you may want to read the book Chase wrote after his intellectual rebirth, *The Tyranny of Words*. This is a light book that doesn't connect strongly with rational self-counselling, but it nevertheless is a rather enjoyable read.

Do you happen to be a parent? Do you plan to be one? Would you like a guidebook on how to teach rational self-counselling to your children and rational parenting to yourself? If so, you're in luck. There are two excellent books available: *The Rational Management of Children* by Paul Hauck, and the more comprehensive *How to Raise an Emotionally Healthy, Happy Child* by Albert Ellis, *et al.* These authors present a convincing case that rational thinking can be taught to children at an early age. This seems obvious to me. Children have mastered the basic irrational ideas of our culture by about eight years. I see no reason to believe that sane ideas based on evidence and logic are any harder to learn or accept than nonsense. You will, however, need guidance on how to teach these concepts to your children; so buy these valuable books if you're a parent.

Would you like some self-help materials geared to humour? Everybody's favourite in this genre is *A Garland of Rational Songs*, written and sung by Albert Ellis. The lyrics are set to well known classic tunes and easy to sing. They are available on tape and CD from the Albert Ellis Institute. On one side, Ellis delivers a lecture on the role of humour in rational psychotherapy, and on the other side he sings his delightful songs. I promise you that hearing Albert Ellis sing is a memorable experience.

If you ever finish reading all these books, you may decide you want a deeper knowledge of rational psychotherapy — its theoretical foundations, its guiding principles, its answers to critics, and so forth. For this deeper and more comprehensive approach, there's an easy pick: *Reason and Emotion in Psychotherapy* by the founding father of rational psychotherapy, Dr Albert Ellis. Of all the books written by Ellis, I believe this is the jewel in his crown. I consider it an indispensable book in my personal library.

I've taken a few potshots at traditional psychotherapy in this book. If such irreverence amuses you, and if you want to pursue a critical look at why traditional psychiatry has missed the boat, you might enjoy The *Death of Psychiatry* by E Fuller Torrey. The author — who is himself a psychiatrist — has taken a tremendous amount of flak because of his maverick views. Not a few shrinks would like to see Torrey's credentials lifted. I recommend this book for pure entertainment, but it will also give you some excellent insights into how Freud put us on the wrong track, and why Albert Ellis has been putting us on the right track.

If you consider yourself an egghead, you might want to delve even deeper into the follies of Freud; in which case you might enjoy reading *Skeptical Engagements*, a collection of essays by Frederick Crews. He does a devastating critique of psychoanalysis and all those who fell for this self-validating doctrine. Crews does a nice job of using psychoanalysis as a classic example of a pseudoscience. I must caution you, however, that his essays are densely intellectual and certainly not for everyone.

As you can tell, I love talking about books, and I could go on indefinitely musing over the many wonderful volumes that have enriched my journey through the world of rational self-counselling, but I trust I've given you sufficient samples to start you down the road. These works, which will usually contain additional reading lists, will launch you on the way to becoming an expert on clear thinking and its connection to a happy life. I hope you'll rigorously undertake the journey. If you do, and you persist, I promise you the rewards will be richer than you ever dreamed possible.

Most books and other materials on rational self-help may be ordered from the Albert Ellis Institute. You also may obtain information on the many wonderful workshops and training classes in REBT sponsored by the Institute. Write to the following address for a catalogue: Albert Ellis Institute, 45 East 65th Street, New York NY 10021 email: orders@rebt.org

Index